International Perspectives on Public Administration

IIIIIIIIIIIIIIIIIIIIIIIIIIII
I0123740

International Perspectives on Public Administration uses civilizational theory for grouping and analyzing systems of public administration in different countries around the world, thus offering a global perspective which reveals how different systems may be divided by cultural borders of the modern day.

The author uses different scientific disciplines – namely political theory, political philosophy, law and economics – to offer comparative analyses of the genesis and development of public administration systems in the Western, Orthodox, Islamic, Confucian, Hindu, Buddhist, Japanese and African civilizations, together with reviewing their experience in application of the most modern and progressive practices of public management.

This book will be of great interest to students and scholars of public administration, political science, public management, public policy and civilizational theory.

Henry T. Sardaryan is Doctor Habilitatus in Political Science, Dean of the School of Governance and Politics at MGIMO University – Moscow State Institute of International Relations, Russia, and Official Representative of the Russian Federation at the United Nations Committee of Experts of Public Administration.

Innovations in International Affairs
Series Editor: Raffaele Marchetti
LUISS Guido Carli, Italy

Innovations in International Affairs aims to provide cutting-edge analyses of controversial trends in international affairs with the intent to innovate our understanding of global politics. Hosting mainstream as well as alternative stances, the series promotes both the re-assessment of traditional topics and the exploration of new aspects.

The series invites both engaged scholars and reflective practitioners, and is committed to bringing non-western voices into current debates.

Innovations in International Affairs is keen to consider new book proposals in the following key areas:

- **Innovative topics**: related to aspects that have remained marginal in scholarly and public debates
- **International crises**: related to the most urgent contemporary phenomena and how to interpret and tackle them
- **World perspectives**: related mostly to non-western points of view

Titles in this series include:

Value Chains Transformation and Transport Reconnection in Eurasia
Geo-economic and Geopolitical Implications
Jacopo Maria Pepe

After Theory: How Not to Think About Praxis in Politics
Friedrich Kratochwil

International Perspectives on Public Administration
Henry T. Sardaryan

For more information about this series, please visit: www.routledge.com/ Innovations-in-International-Affairs/book-series/IIA

International Perspectives on Public Administration

Henry T. Sardaryan

Routledge
Taylor & Francis Group

LONDON AND NEW YORK

First published 2021
by Routledge
2 Park Square, Milton Park, Abingdon, Oxon OX14 4RN

and by Routledge
605 Third Avenue, New York, NY 10158

Routledge is an imprint of the Taylor & Francis Group, an informa business

© 2021 Henry T. Sardaryan

The right of Henry T. Sardaryan to be identified as author of this
work has been asserted by him in accordance with sections 77 and
78 of the Copyright, Designs and Patents Act 1988.

All rights reserved. No part of this book may be reprinted
or reproduced or utilised in any form or by any electronic,
mechanical, or other means, now known or hereafter invented,
including photocopying and recording, or in any information
storage or retrieval system, without permission in writing from the
publishers.

Trademark notice: Product or corporate names may be trademarks
or registered trademarks, and are used only for identification and
explanation without intent to infringe.

British Library Cataloguing-in-Publication Data
A catalogue record for this book is available from the British Library

Library of Congress Cataloging-in-Publication Data
Names: Sardaryan, Henry T., author.
Title: International perspectives on public administration /
    Henry T. Sardaryan.
Description: Abingdon, Oxon ; New York, NY : Routledge,
    2021. | Series: Innovations in international affairs | Includes
    bibliographical references and index.
Identifiers: LCCN 2020053808 (print) | LCCN 2020053809
    (ebook) | ISBN 9780367641726 (hardback) | ISBN
    9781003123361 (ebook)
Subjects: LCSH: Public administration—Philosophy. |
    Comparative government.
Classification: LCC JF1351 .S323 2021 (print) | LCC JF1351
    (ebook) | DDC 351.01—dc23
LC record available at https://lccn.loc.gov/2020053808
LC ebook record available at https://lccn.loc.gov/2020053809

ISBN: 978-0-367-64172-6 (hbk)
ISBN: 978-0-367-64184-9 (pbk)
ISBN: 978-1-003-12336-1 (ebk)

Typeset in Times New Roman
by Apex CoVantage, LLC

Contents

Introduction

This book is devoted to public administration, a relatively new field of study that has become extremely important for our country. Traditionally, matters related to the constitution and operation of government and its relations with society have been the center of attention for both national and international scholars.

However, these matters have typically been treated in a universalistic manner. Having first appeared as a theoretical concept in the West, public administration was perceived for a long time as a technocratic system depending upon legal regulation and socio-economic conditions. But today's world clearly demonstrates that civilizational affiliation and cultural legacy are among the most important factors when it comes to assessing whether a given country has the necessary basis for the formation and operation of governmental institutions.

This book deals with the comparative analysis of public administration systems in countries belonging to different civilizations and is aimed at identifying the in-depth reasons for which they have taken their present forms. Having reviewed its contents, would-be public administrators will get a consistent understanding of the key trends in public administration all over the world and of the experience accumulated not only by the leading nations but also by some developing countries in reforming their own political and governance systems.

The problem of structuring the activities of governmental bodies is now viewed not only from the perspective of enhancing the convenience of public services being offered to citizens but also as one of the factors that could contribute to the growth of the economy, which is vitally dependent upon an environment promoting the attraction of investments and the development of innovations. As times passes, it becomes increasingly obvious that a mere reduction in the number of public servants will not always solve the problems at hand, and the development of the nation strongly requires breakthrough growth.

On the other hand, it is not only public civil servants who need to study the basic principles of government operation. Irrespective of whether you work for a federal ministry or a corporation, the system of public administration directly affects you. Understanding the mechanisms and logic of its evolution is an important component of a manager's professional competence in any area. And, when it comes to international experience and foreign systems, knowledge of this kind would be almost unique.

1 The theoretical principles of public administration

1.1 The concept and essence of public administration

Public administration as a phenomenon has existed since the time when the first state came into being, because it, in its essence, is inextricably linked to the need to exercise authority and manage society. In each country, it has its own specific features and is embodied and implemented in various forms, but no state could exist without a system of public administration.

Whereas the state and power have been of interest to philosophers for millennia, public administration as a separate field of scholarly knowledge has started to evolve rather recently. Globalization and the instant distribution of information, as well as the openness and transparency of the contemporary world, have made it clear that, despite the similar configurations occurring in the legal regulation of government forms or in the territorial and political constitution of countries, the operating efficiency of public authorities and their specific features and structures are totally different in the various parts of the world.

As a field of scholarly research and academic discipline, public administration combines fundamental knowledge from various sciences. One cannot imagine it without *jurisprudence*, which contains knowledge regarding law, the only framework within which public authorities operate in the majority of contemporary efficient states. In its turn, *political science* provides today's public administration with ideas regarding the origin and political nature of public authorities and the specific features of their functioning in various civilizational and cultural environments. Finally, *economics* fills public administration with knowledge allowing us to, for example, evaluate the performance of public authorities, process and analyze statistical data and develop and implement various strategies of economic policy.

Before discussing the concept and substance of public administration, it should be noted that its configuration and operating principles take very different shapes in the various countries of the contemporary world. At the same time, the pioneers in the theoretical conceptualization of public administration were, as a rule, European philosophers, who tried to ascribe a universal nature to the patterns and established traditions of public administration in European countries – a trend that still prevails, not only in many contemporary studies, but also even in some international standards and directives.

Nevertheless, whatever part of the world a state is located in, it needs the staff, powers and resources to exercise its authority. The term "public administration" includes two parts – "administration", which refers to the substance of the activity, and "public", which refers to its nature.

It should also be noted that in English, for instance, the idea of running something could be conveyed by at least three terms – "administration", "management" and "governance". They are not synonyms, and they represent different approaches toward the exercise of authority. Given that the science of administration has been developed mainly in Western countries, one should consider these terms in order to understand the underlying notions.

The concept of *administration* refers to the systematic process of running an organization based on certain functions intended to prepare plans, define policies and procedures, set goals and tasks and enforce rules and regulations.

In its turn, *management* means directing people and their work to achieve a common goal using the resources of the relevant organization by means of creating an environment in which the manager and his or her subordinates can work together toward a common goal.

Finally, *governance* refers to the running of a social system (family, formal or informal organization, region or nation) through the processes of interaction and decision-making among the actors involved in collective problem solving that eventually leads to the creation, reinforcement or reproduction of social norms and institutions.

Therefore, the very contents of the notion "administration/management/governance" depend upon the specific form of its operation, the roles of participants in the process and the set of its actors' functions and powers.

However, there exists a common thing consolidating the various forms of administration/management/governance, that is, the idea of leadership being exercised through the making, implementing and following-up of any decisions aimed at achieving the objectives and tasks at hand.

The creation and reproduction of various forms of administration in social relationships are inherent in humankind. A family, a sports training group, a school, a university, a corporate staff, a district, a city, a region or a country as a whole represent various social systems that require very diverse forms of administration in order to run them.

Of course, public administration is the most complicated, multi-tiered and regulated large-scale system; it differs from other systems in that the state through its various bodies and their representatives, and acts as the subject of administration, and there exist a number of other differences as well.

Subject (Latin *subjectum* "lying under; being in the base") is the carrier of activity, consciousness and cognition who obtains knowledge of the external world (object) and influences it in the subject's practical activity.

The subject of administration means any person or entity influencing the relevant object in his/her/its practical activity.

Public administration covers the territory of the entire country, region, city or district, depending on the level of the relevant subject of administration. That is, any decisions being made by a state or municipal authority will be binding upon any residents or entities belonging to the territory or field of its competence. Administration in the private sector suggests that any decisions will only be binding upon the staff of the relevant entity.

Public administration in developed countries operates by means of regulatory acts and is based on the supremacy of law principles. Of course, humankind also knows states where the leader's personal decisions, religious principles or tribal traditions prevail over legal regulation. But the systems of public administration in such countries never demonstrate high stability or performance. Regarding the private sector, the decisions being made by an entity's governing bodies do not constitute laws or regulations and can be issued in oral form, and failure to comply with them will not, in most cases, entail criminal or administrative responsibility.

Public administration involves the lawful capability of using force, for example wherever the law is breached, public order is destabilized or the constitutional system is under threat of destruction. Administration in the private sector rules out the use of force with respect to the object of administration in any form whatsoever.

The purpose of public administration is to resolve problems and achieve results aimed at the development of the country, the fulfillment of the strategy determined by its political leadership and the stable and efficient activities of the public authorities. One could also mention such goals as improving the living standards of the population and enhancing the level of security, education and social protection of the citizens; these are, as a rule, indispensable goals for public administration systems in the developed countries of the world. However, humankind has seen in the past and still sees certain totalitarian systems of government, which consider their own reproduction their principal goal, pursue the policy of restraining the development of human potential and use repressive measures to limit the rights and freedoms of their own citizens. They all feature characteristics of a public administration system and constitute such systems, but they are aimed not at the development of the nation, but solely at their own reproduction. At the same time, the principal goal of administration in the private sector is typically the extraction of profit.

Therefore, *public administration* should be understood as the activities of public authorities and their representatives aimed at achieving the goals and objectives determined by the political leadership of the country, such activities being carried out through legal regulation and including certain functions for policy implementation and follow-up, as well as for the provision of any necessary services for the population.

Due to the increasing significance of the activities of public authorities and the need to improve their performance, the *theory of public administration* has started to evolve. This theory is a synthesis of historical science, organizational theory, sociology, political science and related studies and focuses on the meaning, structure and functions of public administration in all of its forms.

Three different approaches toward the understanding of public administration can be distinguished in contemporary science and practice: Public Administration, New Public Management and Public Governance.

Long before Max Weber had formulated the key principles governing the formation of national bureaucracy, which still constitute the basis for the activities of a public administration system in most contemporary countries, nepotism-free bureaucracy models emerged in a number of countries worldwide.

Nepotism is a system based on giving advantages to relatives in various fields, including business, politics, entertainment, sports, religion and other activities.

When in the 500s B.C. China made the transition from the aristocratic principle of manning its military forces (mainly the cavalry) to the formation of a large infantry recruited from the poorer strata of its population, that change resulted in the need to mobilize more resources through the collection of taxes, that, it its turn, required a bureaucratic staff based on the principle of an employee's maximum efficiency rather than his belonging to a given family.

But Max Weber was the first to systematize the key principles of bureaucratic organization in a state. He was convinced that bureaucracy was the most efficient and rational way to organize human activity and that systematic processes and organized hierarchies are necessary to maintain order, maximize efficiency and eliminate favoritism.

Maximilian Carl Emil Weber (April 21, 1864, Erfurt, Prussia– June 14, 1920, Munich, Germany) was a German sociologist, philosopher, historian and political economist.

Bureaucracy (from French *bureau* "bureau, office" + Greek κράτος "domination, power") is a body of non-electable public servants working for public authorities.

Weber believed that legitimacy-based rational domination embodied in an authority relying upon a law or norm would be increasingly prevailing in society, thus leading to the formation of a bureaucracy.[1] A bureaucratic administration means, in his opinion, domination by force of knowledge, on the basis of rationality. Weber believed that the principal source for the supremacy of the bureaucratic administration was technical knowledge that, through the development of modern technology and economic methods in production, had become absolutely necessary to public servants.

One can identify the following key characteristic features of bureaucracy as discussed in Weber's works:

1 The existence of certain services and, consequently, competencies are strictly regulated by law, with clear separation and distribution of functions among public servants, as well as the necessary decision-making powers in order to fulfill such tasks;
2 Employees are protected in exercising their functions by virtue of law (for instance, the irremovable status of judges);
3 The nature of work is full-time, in contrast to the concept of public service as a sort of hobby carried out concurrently with some other types of work, which was typical for the earlier stages of society's evolution;
4 The functions of state power are characterized by strict hierarchy, which suggests a highly structured administrative system, with superior and subordinate units, a vertical organization of staff and the need for a lower level to approach a higher one;
5 Staff is to be recruited on a competitive basis, with certain requirements and criteria being applied to candidates, and any employee is to be

appointed (or, rarely, elected) on the basis of selection and contractual undertakings;

6   An employee's remuneration is a fixed amount and includes a pension entitlement after retirement; the salary varies in accordance with the internal hierarchy of administration and the significance of the functions the employee performs;

7   The government is entitled to supervise the activities of public servants, including by setting up disciplinary committees;

8   Public servants are eligible for promotion according to objective criteria rather than by discretion of the political leadership;

9   Any function is completely separate from the person performing it, because no employee may be the owner of his or her office or means of administration.

In a classical hierarchy, the organization head in a governmental body, as a rule, has several deputies, each of whom coordinates the operations of several divisions consisting of departments that include offices (Figure 1.1).

It should be noted that such an organizational chart in governmental bodies, as well as in the private sector, continues to exist in most countries worldwide. Despite the fact that new models of cross-functional or project management have been developed, the traditional distribution of hierarchy

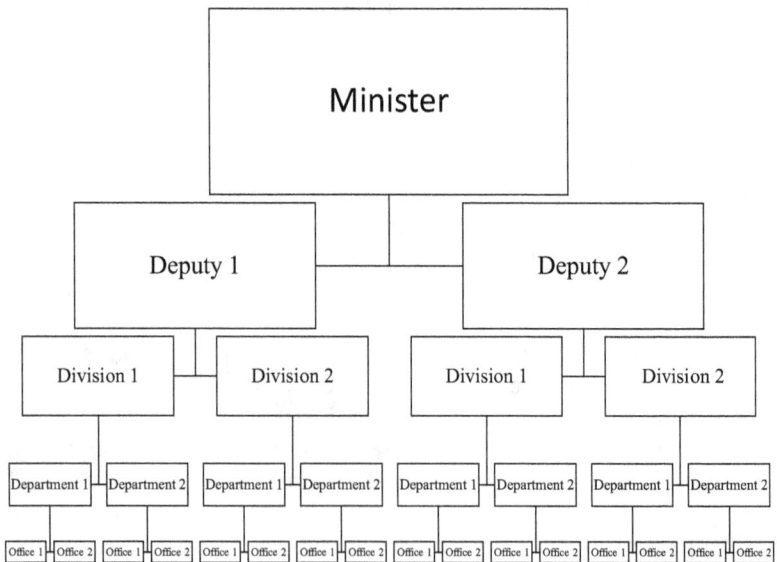

Figure 1.1 Organizational Chart in Governmental Bodies

in accordance with functional subordination and its vertical organization still remains the most common configuration of a bureaucratic system globally.

Figures 1.2 and 1.3 are given as examples.

A system of this kind has both strengths and obvious weaknesses. Strict hierarchy and centralization are primarily required to follow up the implementation of decisions and the strict observance of their deadlines and involve the high personal responsibility of employees. Centralization and vertical subordination enable governmental staff to maintain an uninterrupted and stable process of administration.

On the other hand, public administration structured in this way involves an extremely time-consuming procedure for coordination among offices

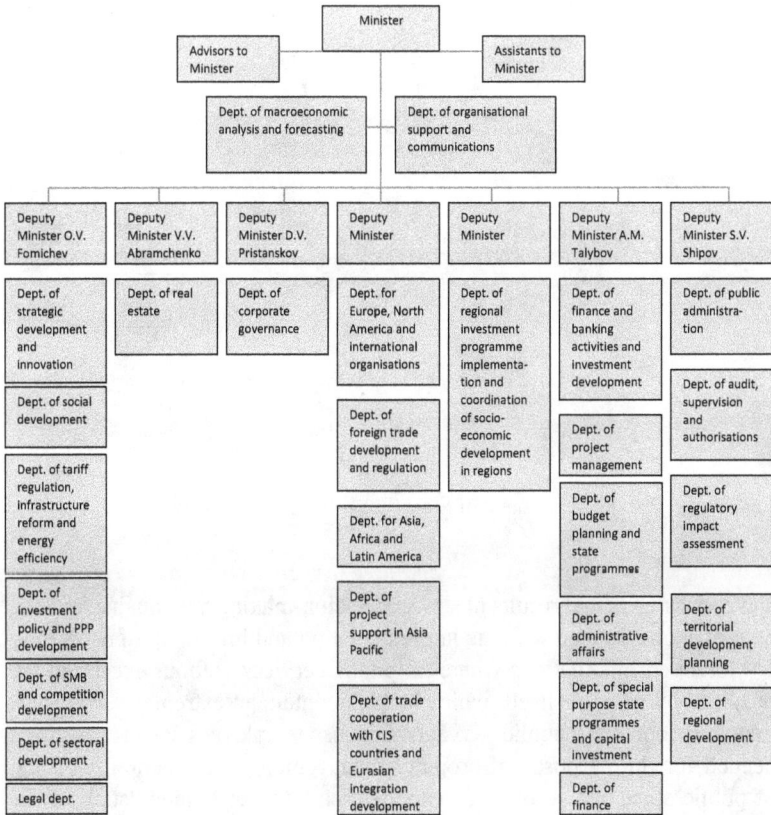

Figure 1.2 Russian Ministry of Economics

Figure 1.3 The US Department of State

and departments that results in slower decision-making and much excessive paperwork associated with the implementation and follow-up of decisions.

Moreover, in situations where all public services without exception are provided by the state itself, which has to maintain an extremely large staff, including not only public servants but also employees of various sorts needed for the purposes of property management, construction, cleaning of public areas and so on, the costs of such "budget-funded" staff can be excessive for the state. The efficiency and quality of the relevant services are strongly questioned as well.

Questions for self-study:

1 Please consider the implementation of a social security reform by using knowledge from jurisprudence, political science and economics. Why should a public administrator know all of the three fields of science well?
2 Please review the structure of the Ministry of Economic Development. Please describe the functions of its subdivisions.
3 Please examine the structure of an executive body in the government of Singapore.

Additional literature:

European Commission. *Quality of Public Administration. A Toolbox for Practitioners.* Directorate-General for Employment, Social Affairs and Inclusion Unit E.1. 2015
Juneja, P. *Structural Functional Approach to Public Administration.* Management Study Guide. 2019
Weber, M. The Three Types of Legitimate Rule. *Berkeley Publications in Society and Institutions.* 1958. Vol. 4 (1)

1.2 New Public Management and public governance

The term "New Public Management" (NPM) was invented by British scholar Christopher Hood, who proposed to take a new look at organizational structure in the public sector. Now NPM has exceeded the limits outlined by Hood, and a vast number of scholars use it to examine, for example, a new model of institutional economics or changes in policy development procedures.

The changes that shaped NPM began to occur in the 1980s, first in the UK, where an attempt was made to replicate certain technologies and mechanisms from the field of business in the public sector in order to enhance its efficiency and to implement a management model characteristic of the private sector.

NPM also suggested more decentralized resource control and using alternative models for service provision to achieve higher results, including a quasi-market structure in which public and private service providers would compete with each other for the right to offer public services.

One could name the following key characteristics of NPM:

1 Strong emphasis on financial control, the price/quality ratio and improving the performance of public services;
2 The team- and control-based mode of operation, the definition and setting of objectives and continuous performance monitoring;

3   The implementation of audits at both the financial and professional levels, the use of transparent tools for performance evaluation and the setting of performance indicators;
4   A wider use of client-driven solutions;
5   A higher volume of contracts undertaken by providers from the non-public sector;
6   The implementation of new forms for corporate governance and a model based on the operation of a board of directors.

The system clearly benefited from so-called outsourcing, where the state delegates certain groups of its functions to the private sector, that, given the competition for the right to undertake them, results in the selection of those providers who are willing to work for the lowest price and with the highest quality.

It should be taken into account, however, that NPM can only be used in the presence of a full-fledged business community ensuring competition for contracts and of a well-established legal system capable of guaranteeing the transparency of the relevant procedures and the provider's compliance with its obligations.

In many countries, where NPM was viewed as a panacea for all problems of public administration and, therefore, used without due regard for economic and business reality, it has only resulted in the growth of corruption risks, the state's avoidance of responsibility in extremely sensitive social areas and further deterioration of service quality.

NPM was initially implemented in the UK, New Zealand, the US and Scandinavia in the mid-1980s. Its philosophy is based on the idea that individual personal interest determines bureaucratic behavior. NPM has led to significant changes in the spirit and approach of the public sector, especially as regards the implementation of new management methods, the outsourcing of basic services to the private sector by means of contracts, an enhanced focus on results and so on.

Outsourcing means an agreement under which one entity appoints another entity to carry out a certain activity that is or might be performed by the former entity itself.

In public administration, **outsourcing** refers to the practice of delegating the provision of public services to private businesses.

That being said, the implementation of NPM in non-European countries, despite large-scale international support, has produced contradictory results. Despite the fact that the model itself claimed a universal nature and replicability irrespective of the environment in which it was used, practice has demonstrated that only some of its elements and mechanisms have been implemented in the public administration systems of developing countries. They put principal emphasis on establishing public authorities similar to those which operated in the UK, such as executive agencies and autonomous tax authorities.

Outsourcing in the fields of public health, education and water supply has become a rather widespread practice, but the quality of the relevant services, legal regulation and the efficiency of the new public authorities still raise significant doubts among the experts.

Currently, Public Governance (PG) is indicated as a new stage in the development of public administration in the UN Development Program and the policy documents of the OSCE, the European Union and some other organizations.

Regarding its meaning, the term "governance" refers to governing by means of law-making, policy definition, debates and broad public discussions. In this context, governance is a higher level of management in relation to administration, which refers to operational regulation, control and service provision.

PG concentrates on the implementation of formal and informal arrangements that determine how public decisions are made and how public actions are carried out, from the perspective of maintaining a country's constitutional values when facing changing problems and environments. The principal elements of PG are accountability, transparency, efficiency, effectiveness and rule of law.

The mechanisms of PG help build trust and provide stability needed for planning investment in the medium and long term; they transform interaction between the state and the general public by replacing the "control and command" approach with more flexible principles in guidance, communication and persuasion.

PG includes several key principles of implementation:

1   Regulatory reform framework;
2   Coordination across government;
3   Regulatory impact analysis;
4   Public consultation;
5   Simplifying the administrative burden.

Let us discuss these five elements in more detail.

Regulatory reform framework

Regulatory policy is the process by which regulations and standards are drafted, updated, implemented and enforced. Regulations, which encourage market development, innovation and competitiveness, improve economic performance.

Inefficient regulation can, on the contrary, slow down business development, divert resources away from investments, hamper entry into international markets, reduce jobs and so on. The predictability of regulatory policy and guarantees of its implementation in practice are the key factors, failing which it is impossible to achieve investor confidence.

Reform involves the determination of exact deadlines, goals and mechanisms for evaluating its results. It cannot be implemented without political support from the country's leadership. The implementation of measurable regulatory quality standards is very important for the purposes of reform.

The process in itself will not have any completion point and requires improving the regulatory potential of governance on a continuous basis. Moreover, no reform will be efficient if it focuses solely on the creation of new regulations without reviewing and updating the existing ones.

One of the principal ways to push reform forward is the adoption of new regulatory tools through legal reform reducing the excessive discretion of regulators and providers, including a wide use of public consultation.

Coordination across government

In most countries, PG has a multi-level structure and is characterized by both the distribution of functions among departments at the national level and the allocation of regional authorities, as well as municipal authorities, the latter not being part of government but significantly influencing the regulation of public relationships.

In this situation, even the most efficient decisions of particular authorities can be compromised by the poor quality of regulation at other levels or within parallel institutions, adversely affecting investment and economic performance. The most common problems that affect the relations between the public and the private sectors are the duplication of functions and overlapping responsibility.

To address this issue, certain key principles and practices have been developed for ensuring coherent regulation and facilitating coordination among institutions at different levels of government. Efficient coordination requires a clear definition of regulatory powers, which avoids overlapping responsibilities, together with negotiation mechanisms to surmount decision-making divergences. All parts of central government – the executive branch, the legislative branch and the judiciary – have key roles to play in supporting the regulatory quality process, but the executive is typically the most active regulator.

In most cases, institutional coordination mechanisms derive from constitutional arrangements, but there are also informal coordination tools that facilitate the design and implementation of regulatory policy. Some countries have established permanent discussion tables and ad hoc conferences that promote dialogue between the central and lower levels of government, as well as the industry-specific departments of the executive.

In order to facilitate communication and transparency and improve regulatory clarity and coherence, it is also helpful to simplify and codify legislation, to create registers of existing and proposed regulations and to use information technology to secure access to regulatory material.

It should also be taken into account that certain areas may be subject to regulation not only at the national or sub-national level, but also at the supra-national (international) level, which directly necessitates ongoing harmonization between national standards and international rules.

Regulatory impact analysis

Regulatory impact analysis examines and measures the likely benefits, shortcomings and overall effects of new or changed regulations. It provides decision-makers with valuable empirical data and a comprehensive framework to assess options and the possible social and economic consequences of their decisions.

Regulatory impact analysis is applied differently in each regulatory system, depending on priorities and context. There are, however, certain basic elements without which it would be impossible:

1   Define the policy context and identify the problem that triggers action by government;
2   Identify and define all possible regulatory and non-regulatory options that could achieve the policy objective, including doing nothing;
3   Identify and quantify costs and benefits for each option;
4   Design enforcement and compliance strategies for each option, including an evaluation of their effectiveness and efficiency;

Compliance refers to that part of an organization's governance system which deals with the risks of failure to fulfill the requirements of any laws or regulations or of any rules or standards issued by supervisory authorities, industry associations or self-regulatory organizations.

5   Develop monitoring mechanisms to evaluate the success of the policy proposal in achieving its objectives and feed that information into the development of future regulatory measures.

Public consultation

Communicating information on regulatory decisions to the public has currently become a key building block of the rule of law. At an initial stage, as a rule, it takes the shape of a one-way process of communication in which the public is treated as a passive consumer of government information. Whereas such communication does not, by itself, constitute consultation, it can be a first step.

Consultation involves actively seeking the opinions of interest groups affected by the proposed regulation. Now it is a two-way flow of information, which may occur at any stage of regulatory development, from problem identification to evaluation of existing regulation. This option requires not just passive awareness from the interest groups but also active participation in the formulation of regulatory objectives, policies and approaches in regulatory development.

Consultation may be informal, including all forms of contacts between regulators and interest groups. The most basic tool is the circulation of regulatory proposals for public discussion. This procedure increasingly uses not only such conventional means as printed media, radio or television but also internet platforms, social media networks and other online resources.

There is an established practice of public consultation such as hearings, which can be hosted either by public authorities (such as parliamentary hearings involving representatives of interest groups) or by the interest groups themselves (business associations, chambers of commerce and industry, etc.).

Simplifying the administrative burden

Administrative simplification is the most commonly used regulatory reform tool. It focuses on reducing and streamlining procedural formalities and paperwork in the public sector. As a rule, reform of this type starts with a reduction in the scope of permits and licenses required by supervisory authorities. An administrative burden disadvantageous to the development of small- and medium-sized businesses quite often drives them into a so-called shadow, thus reducing tax payments to the state budget and distorting statistical data on the number of employees, the volume of transactions and so on.

In order to simplify administrative procedures, one should be guided by the real situation in the country and the society and take into account the specific features of development in the economy, but this process would be rather unfeasible without a number of key steps.

First, it is necessary not only to modify the form in which certain functions are implemented by the government but also, and primarily, to review and re-engineer the entire governance process. It should be understood whether a given government function is necessary at all. What problem is to be solved with the help of the required form of reporting?

Process re-engineering is based on the review of information requirements for government formalities in order to optimize them and reduce their number and the burden they impose on businesses and citizens. The increasingly popular practice of so-called single-window services (or "one-stop shops") eliminates the need to visit dozens of different departments in order to obtain required documents, because the entire process of their processing and issuance is concentrated in a single multifunctional center.

The "silence = consent" principle, providing for a tacit mechanism of approval of applications once a fixed period of time expires, is often used for authorizations. That is, if the relevant public authority has failed to express its objection or denial, the decision will be deemed to be made automatically.

These and other measures are part of the e-government model, which goes far beyond simple electronic dissemination of documents. The governments of many contemporary countries increasingly use information technology to reduce bureaucratic procedures, primarily by offering such tools as online data filing, online one-stop shops and e-procurement.

Questions for self-study:

1   Please examine the experience of Margaret Thatcher's government in the UK in reforming public services.
2   Please identify the top five most successful countries in the application of New Public Management mechanisms. Please examine the key stages of modifications in the systems of public administration in these countries.
3   Please review the regulatory impact of any decisions made by the RF government during the past year.

Additional literature:

Chandler, J. and M. Dent. *Questioning the New Public Management*. Taylor & Francis Limited. 2019

Torfing, J., L.B. Andersen, K.K. Klausen and C. Greve. *Public Governance Paradigms: Competing and Co-Existing*. Edward Elgar Publishing, Incorporated. 2020
UNDP. *From Old Public Administration to the New Public Service*. UNDP. 2015

1.3 Political culture and public administration

During the 20th century, the world was, in ideological terms, divided into the capitalist and the Communist camps. After the fall of the Berlin Wall and the breakdown of the Soviet Union, there was an increasingly popular belief that any form of global conflict would be ruled out in the future and that humankind would inevitably embrace a uniform political model at both the national and the supra-national levels. That process was supposed to influence the system of government in all parts of the world as well.

The scientific literature that was issued after the 1990s tried to use all possible ways to build a linear timeline logic to describe the evolution of government models in the various countries of the world; such logic was to include uniform stages and features and the only alternative for the future.

The liberal political ideology, its model and its values claimed a universal status, but they have clearly failed to cope with this role. After the bipolar division of humankind was eliminated, the world has proved unable to pass a new civilizational watershed.

Western values have failed to become universal, because, due to their Western origin, they are essentially Christian in nature. An attempt to build Europe based on so-called secular humanism instead of the Christian civilizational heritage is now in an acute phase of crisis featuring an array of attributes. The inability to integrate immigrants, the dilution of the family, the deterioration of education and so on are social manifestations of an identity crisis resulting from Jacobin-style secularization.

The Jacobins refers to the best-known political movement of the Great French Revolution named after the seat of its meetings, the monastery of the Jacobins in Rue Saint-Jacques in Paris. The movement believed that the idea of secular government meant the need to completely destroy the Christian legacy and church institutions.

The transformation described in the preceding paragraph has largely been reflected in the key documents of the UN, the Council of Europe, the OSCE and other organizations, which ascribe a universal status to the key elements of the modern Western model and, consequently, call other countries to embrace similar models of government.

It is obvious, however, that in order to implement, for instance, a mechanism of public consultation, one could plan to adopt dozens of laws and regulations determining a procedure for government consultation with representatives of interest groups, their direct involvement in regulatory development and so on, but any steps along this line would be absolutely senseless unless such interest groups exist in the form of established and independent public associations, which could also be referred to as civic society.

The same can be said about the majority of other principles and mechanisms of public administration in Western countries, which are based on the social and economic processes that have taken place in those countries and enabled the formation of the key institutions that have predetermined the circle of actors, the pattern of their relations and the setting of goals within the system of government.

In this regard, the question is: what is the watershed or key factor that determines the course of social, economic, public and political processes in the various countries of the world? The significance of political culture as the basis for the functioning of a political system is rarely questioned in today's political discourse and more and more often inspires investigations into the reasons for the formation of various economic models and even the reasons for differences in the rates of economic growth among various countries.

Nevertheless, a large number of issues related to the notion, substance and origin of political culture still remain open. As a rule, this matter comes under consideration in an attempt to identify patterns of political behavior, to explain the ability or inability to achieve political mobilization or the propensity for various ideologies, but very rarely to review the relationship between culture and the genesis of political institutions.

In 1973, American sociologist Clifford Geertz defined culture as

> a historically transmitted picture of meanings embodied in symbols, a system of inherited conceptions expressed in symbolic forms by means of which men communicate, perpetuate and develop their knowledge about and attitudes toward life.[2]

Luigi Guiso, Paola Sapienza and Luigi Zingales offered one of the most common definitions; they state that political culture refers to those customary beliefs and values that ethnic, religious and social groups transmit from generation to generation.[3]

An important contribution to the study of culture, including political culture, was a work by Gabriel Almond, in which he defined it as the "particular pattern of orientations to political action that is inherent in each political system". In a later work, *Civic Culture*, Almond, together with Sidney Verba, proposed a detailed systematic review of political culture, the first of its kind.[4]

One characteristic of the work is that the authors view the culture of a society as the aggregate of values of its constituent individuals. Contemporary researchers supporting this approach, such as Antiseri and Infantino, bring individualism in their society studies to an extreme point by affirming that there exist neither classes nor society as such, but only individuals.[5]

But this is not the only paradigm of its kind. An alternative concept treats society as consisting of individuals but not being their mere aggregate. Society is an integral phenomenon living its own life, which cannot be reduced to the existence of the people it consists of; it is an entity that evolves according to its own laws. Whereas the former approach can be called sociological individualism, the latter is often labeled by the term "sociological realism". For example, French sociologist Durkheim, who noted that the society was a reality independent from its individuals, was a prominent supporter of sociological realism.[6]

Most modern investigations into political culture and its impact on political systems are limited to reviewing changes in the political behavior of individuals and society under the influence of any given culture or the degree of political involvement.

By no means denying the importance of individuals' political preferences and electoral behavior, I believe that this issue is secondary in relation to the genesis of political institutions that this approach effectively omits to address. Western science considers the origin of public institutions primarily within the paradigm of liberal idealism and legal positivism, limiting its discourse to the perfection of legal regulation, constitutional guarantee mechanisms and so on, and missing the key significance of the political culture that has led to their formation.

One could discuss specific political preferences of citizens in those countries that may result in the election of leaders supporting political ideologies uncommon to the West, but this cannot explain the configuration of relations across the entire system of government either. Moreover, these preferences in themselves are not limited solely to the degree of public involvement. Modern Western democracies have seen the election of political leaders challenging the entire conceptual basis of their functioning, but that has never resulted in the breakdown of the system as such, leading at most to the restructuring of particular mechanisms and configurations of relations among its components – for instance, to the modification of party systems and election laws.

The origin of the social institutions underlying the political ones is of key significance. Where social institutions of a specific kind are non-existent, a Western model of government will either operate formally or soon cease to operate at all, giving way to power distribution and exercise mechanisms more traditional for the society. And in this case, culture and, accordingly, political culture will acquire key importance.

The most important elements under the influence of political culture are as follows:

1   The mechanism for the formation of political power;
2   The personified or institutional nature of political power;
3   Functional separation of power;
4   Territorial separation of power;
5   Effective accountability of government;
6   Arrangements allowing for rotation in power while preserving the political system;
7   The existence of non-governmental institutions in the society that influence the political process;
8   The supremacy of law.

It is clear that all eight items are interrelated and cannot operate without each other. For example, rotation in power would not work without electability, even in the case of monarchy, which should be limited for this purpose. In this case, we can also speak about the accountability of government, which, in its turn, depends upon its functional separation. The latter cannot be implemented if power is personified, and its institutional nature can only be guaranteed by the supremacy of law, which rules out any change in the "rules of play" during the play process. The contemporary world knows many examples of government models featuring two or three of the aforementioned principles, but those systems either suffer from permanent crisis or falsify democratic institutions due to the absence of the other elements.

It should be noted that the principles referred to previously are just the typical foundations of the contemporary Western model of democracy, but they do not constitute any universal values that should necessarily be at the core of any state. But if the leaders, the public or international organizations prefer to use the Western model of democracy to build a system of government, then the existence of a political culture implying the functioning of such institutions is an indispensable condition. Simply speaking, if a given African country adopts an exact copy of the French Constitution, it will require French political culture and, accordingly, the social institutions to make it work.

Therefore, *political culture* can be understood as the system of values inherent in a society which is transmitted from generation to generation and shapes attitudes toward political institutions, processes and mechanisms of power exercise.

In order to answer the question about the basis of political culture, one should discuss the key component of this phenomenon: values. As supposed by all approaches, whether liberal or realistic, it is values that constitute the code shaping a society's attitude toward any matter, including those belonging to the domain of public administration.

Political science has developed the concept of so-called altruistic voting, as opposed to electoral egoism. It is based on the idea of a voter behavior model, in which citizens in a democratic society give preference to "social" voting over an extremely low probability of egoistic voting. In this case, the collective interest of the society outweighs the position of a particular individual, who demonstrates a sort of altruism for the sake of the common good. Some scholars say that altruistic voting is similar to a lottery, where the probability of winning a prize is very low, but the prize itself is rather high, so that the anticipated benefit exceeds the costs.

If we go beyond the limits of individuals' electoral behavior and try to extend this concept to the system of government as a whole, it will be clear that any political culture implies a certain altruism on the part of the citizens. If subjective egoism prevailed in this respect, then the whole political life of the society would be limited to the endless manifestation of will to power on the part of its components.

It is clear that this type of society configuration rules out any chance for the society to develop not only democracy but also any other system of political relations. Any society would find itself brought into chaos in a situation where each of its components seeks to gain supreme power and where values are volatile and subject to change solely at the will of those whose power is strongest.

German philosopher Friedrich Nietzsche describes these conditions as characteristics of nihilism, which, in his opinion, will prevail after a moral crisis primarily affecting Christian morality.[7] He is convinced that Christianity itself will result, sooner or later, in nihilism, because the world is incompatible with its ideals.

Nihilism (from Latin *nihil*, "nothing") refers to the theory that puts in doubt the common values, ideals or norms of morality or culture. In the context of Nietzsche's views, to be a nihilist means to realize the illusory and false nature of both the Christian idea of an above-the-world God and the idea of progress.

Nevertheless, a different thing appears to be important here. If reverse logic were applied, then values would be impossible without religion and their absence would eventually lead to chaos. According to Nietzsche, the transition from religion to moralism is merely a phase preceding nihilism, since people do not need to view themselves as the creators of values in the context of religion, and they will inevitably come to nihilism once such a need emerges.

That is, any system of values that is not based on religious culture is a product of human activity and, accordingly, involves potential participation of humankind in the determination of the values, that, given their influence on the system (first of all, on the political system), eliminates any stability or institutionality.

Negatively describing religion and, in particular, Christianity, he demonstrates that its disappearance leads to egoistic chaos, the lack of morality as such and the destruction of any systems, whether political or social. No stable system of public relations can operate without a certain degree of self-sacrifice. From this standpoint, it is also clear that no other ideological basis could be able to set limits to individual egoism and to direct individuals toward the achievement of the common good.

In the absence of any form of the transcendent truth, especially any religious doctrine, no "secular" verification of any decision would be possible, because there would be no criteria for such verification.

Transcendence (from Latin *transcendens*, "going beyond limits") is a philosophic term describing any phenomena which in principle cannot be known from experience.

If such verification relies upon the personal subjective opinion of each individual in a situation where there is no criterion of the common good or ethics, then no decision can be made, because it would be impossible to assess its "secular" correctness.

Secularization is the process of eliminating religion from all areas of public and private life.

Not all decisions being made by political institutions are relevant to the "efficient/inefficient" dilemma. Governments regularly face an ethical choice depending not as much upon the anticipated effectiveness of the proposed decision as upon its appropriateness in terms of conformity with a system of values and beliefs.

That is, if a citizen believes something to be normal in a society where any transcendent truth is non-existent, then the law is the only thing that can prevent him or her from acting unethically. But does it means that, if that citizen manages to gain power and change the law, his or her act will become permissible? If ethics in a society is limited to the individual preferences of its citizens, then no restriction can be imposed.

Moreover, when studying the role of religion in the evolution of political culture, it is important to start the analysis not from the role of spiritual values in an already existing system but from its formation. It is clear that a system of government is not an objective natural phenomenon but rather an abstraction, as are any political or social institutions. This is a system of behavior patterns of individuals and their groups that develops in the field of state power relations. And this system differs from country to country simply due to the influence of political culture. One country may hold elections on a competitive basis, whereas a neighboring country may conduct them formally or not at all. The same is true for the activities of top leadership after an election – the institutional or personified nature of power cannot be explained by the language used in a constitution or legislation, but it stems from the political culture that has shaped this configuration of relations.

The Declaration of Rights of Man and of the Citizen was adopted in France not because the authors were brilliant constitutional lawyers who conceived legal mechanisms for human rights protection for the first time, but because a certain political culture including social institutions, values and beliefs lacked an appropriate legal status at that time. Such a status could have been granted by the monarch, but it is clear that the gap between the then current political culture/political institutions and legal regulation could not have persisted for a long time.

This mechanism cannot be reversed, however. If a society lacks a political culture consistent with democratic rule, then the legal affirmation of such rule and the establishment of any relevant institutions will be merely formal and will result, at best, in the falsification of democratic mechanisms or, in the worst scenario, in a paralyzed government.

When one tries to review the most important components of political culture, it seems easy to identify those factors that are key to the formation of any given model – ethnic, historical, geographic and so on. But in the contemporary world, where information propagates faster than ever, one can observe events and processes in real time on all continents; it becomes increasingly obvious that these factors, while undoubtedly playing their role in the evolution of political culture, are nevertheless secondary in their nature.

For instance, ethnos is usually defined as the aggregate of individual characteristics, which are hard or impossible to modify, such as skin color or main language. The idea that ethnic identify can shape the political views and behavior of people stems from the theory of social identity. This theory provides that any group defines itself vis-à-vis other groups. The human need to create order and ascribe meaning to the social environment makes people differentiate themselves into social groups even in situations where there are no actual differences among such groups.

If we rely upon this concept, then, first, it is evident that the command of a certain language and some physiological features constitute those key characteristics that create a stable association between an individual and a given ethnic group. However, culture, which also belongs to the series of such characteristics, is not a purely ethnic factor. We know many ethnic groups that are very close to each other from a genetic, linguistic and geographic standpoint, but are significantly different in terms of their culture (the Jews and the Arabs, the Serbs and the Croatians, etc.).

The historical factor in itself cannot be an explanation, since the historical evolution of political culture attributes had to involve an in-depth transformation process, whose causation would in any case have an ideological basis.

Geography, as already demonstrated earlier with respect to ethnic differentiation, plays no significant role, and that can be best proved by the fact that a large number of neighboring states in a given region (say, the Middle East or South Asia) with common borders have totally different political cultures and, accordingly, systems of government.

Political culture differs not because of constants that an individual cannot control, such as the color of his or her skin or the geographic area of his or her origin. Nor does it differ because of the linguistic or folklore characteristics of the social group to which the individual belongs. At its core, political culture develops in reliance upon values and beliefs, which are, in turn, determined by religious and cultural heritage.

That being said, one should note that the very notion of "religion" results from Western scientific thought. In the ancient and medieval world, the Latin term "*religio*" was understood as individual worship rather than a doctrine, practice or source of knowledge. In addition, *religio* included broad social obligations to the family, neighbors, rulers and God. The concept of "religion" took its shape during the 16th–17th centuries, despite the fact that the ancient sacred texts, such as the Bible and the Quran, did not include such a notion, and neither the people nor the cultures, in the context of which those sacred texts had been written, were aware of this or any similar term.

Hebrew, for example, knows no exact equivalent of "religion", since Judaism does not draw any clear distinction among religious, ethnic or racial identity. The Greek word "θρησκεία" (*thrēskeía*), used in the New

Testament, is sometimes translated as religion, but this term began to be understood as "worship" only during the medieval period.

In the contemporary translation of the Quran, the Arabic word "*din*" is often translated as religion, but the version "law" was more common until the mid-1600s.

The Sanskrit word "*dharma*", sometimes translated as religion, also means law. In South Asia, the study of law included, inter alia, repentance, piety and sacral ceremonies. In medieval Japan, a similar alliance between the imperial law and the law of Buddha had existed as well, but later they became independent sources.

As concerns the modern abstract concept of religion, its use started largely in the 17th century due to the increasingly active contacts with new civilizations because of geographic discoveries. Until the 19th century, no people identified themselves as Hindu or Buddhist.

Thus, the modern idea of separation between the secular and the clerical, law and religion, serves as the basis for many studies in this area aimed at demonstrating a certain degree of their influence upon each other. In the countries belonging to Christian civilization, the law, including its provisions governing the formation, structure and operation of government, was based on Christian principles and could not substantially contradict them, whereas the non-Christian countries knew, in fact, no separation between secular and religious law.

Therefore, religion can not only determine the beliefs, ethics and values of a particular individual supporting the relevant religious group but also produce a broader system of values, including legal norms that may be identical to the religious principles.

And if religion covered only the matters regulating the spiritual area, as some people often try to claim, then legal norms would also cover only those aspects of human activity: the administration of rites, the operation of worship sites and so on. It is clear, however, that religion, being a connecting link between humankind and metaphysics, regulates the physical world in a deep and detailed manner as well. Marriage, property and labor are typically an integral part of any religious doctrine. And matters related to state power, its organization, its relations with society and the requirements imposed upon it, of course, hold a central place.

Such elements of political culture as the institutional nature of power, the functioning of non-governmental institutions and the functional separation of power are, in fact, heavily dependent upon the role of religious entities in a society.

Given the fact that, over millennia, religion was not perceived as a separate domain of public life, the activities of religious organizations were not perceived the way they are now either. In the contemporary world, the relations between, say, the Catholic Church and the government of the Italian Republic are not only filled with totally different content but also perceived in a radically different way by society and its individuals.

In this regard, the participation of, say, the Catholic Church in the development of law appears to be interesting. It is well known that the baptism of the barbarians heavily impacted their way of life and resulted in a full-scale transformation of their social order. Against that background, German law was experiencing major changes increasingly inspired by Christian doctrine. The Church supports the nomocratic concept of the state and law – a state order in which the ruling elite follow the supremacy of law principle in their political practice. The concept itself stems from Christian doctrine, particularly the epistles of St. Paul, whose theory of divine law involves the universal rule of the law established by God. In this world, an individual's baptism constitutes his or her transition to a new status, including a set of certain rules and duties that are non-existent outside the context of baptism. It is baptism, as the means to acquire a status different from that of "*Homo naturalis*", that imposed the legal obligations on the individual, which he or she, on one hand, could not evade or breach and, on the other hand, in the establishment of which he or she had not participated, because the law, being a divine institution, could not be created by people (*lex est donum Dei*).

This legacy creates an extremely favorable basis for the evolution of a phenomenon that now is usually referred to as the supremacy of law, the rule-of-law state and so on.

An individual's acquiring a status involving a set of rights and duties is in many ways similar to modern citizenship. Without this status, you would also possess certain rights and duties within the territory of the state, but their contents would be very different.

Or, say, the law being established not by government, but by a supreme power, in this case by God, prevents the political leadership from changing the rules of play during the play process, which is an important prerequisite to the operation of the supremacy of law and the rule-of-law nature of the state.

Therefore, the religious and cultural heritage allows one to divide states into relatively homogenous groups in terms of value and cultural characteristics. These groups make it possible to review the common trends and principles of development in various countries.

Such groups or sets of states are identified based on their belonging to a specific *civilization*.

The concept of "civilization" itself is commonly used in two completely different or, as one might say, even mutually exclusive meanings.

One meaning refers to civilization as a stage in the evolution of human society – for example, a transition from barbarism to a civilized society. This approach involves the traditional division of world history into stages and the treatment of humankind's evolution as a linear process directed toward a universal goal, so that some countries make progress along this line while others don't.

But it is obvious that both the historical stages themselves and their time-line parameters correlate with the evolution of public institutions and socio-political processes solely in Europe. Neither the African, nor the Islamic, nor the Latin American societies demonstrated the same configuration of state-society relations as the European ones did within the same periods. Moreover, the very sequence of those formations has never taken place in the history of those societies. When the Middle Ages were in full bloom in Europe, it was hardly possible to find any attributes of a feudal society in Africa, where the transformation of the primitive-communal system into the slavery system and then into the feudal system was never observed in principle.

According to Arnold J. Toynbee, a prominent scholar and a founder of the civilizational approach, societies being "intelligible fields of study" are a genus, within which a particular species can be identified. Toynbee identifies 21 such societies and calls them "civilizations" to distinguish them from primitive societies. He notes that the number of known civilizations is small, whereas the known primitive societies are much more numerous.[8]

Russian sociologist Pitirim Sorokin, criticizing Toynbee's approaches, claimed that civilizations, as the British scholar understood them, were mere conglomerates of various civilizational phenomena and objects united by mere contiguity in space but devoid of causal or meaningful ties, rather than integrated systems.[9] For this reason, as Sorokin believed, they do not constitute genuine social species; so we should not treat them as units and can hardly see any similarity in the processes of their genesis, growth and decline.

A number of scholars have also drawn our attention to one peculiarity: there was a certain limited period of time that contained, concurrently, the preachment of the principal Hebrew prophets during the exile; the development of science and philosophy from Thales to Aristotle in Greece; the evolution of political philosophy from Confucius to the legists in China; and the emergence of religious philosophy in the form of the Upanishads in India.

German philosopher Karl Jaspers proposed to call that period (800–200 B.C.) in the history of humankind the "Axial Age", during which the myth-based worldview had given way to the rational one that shaped the type of human being we still observe.[10] In his opinion, all theories of the Axial Age, which have survived until now in one or another form, are rational and reflect the human intention to rethink pre-existing norms, customs or traditions. At the same time, Jaspers notes that some pre-Axial civilizations (Ancient Egypt, the Assyrian-Babylonian civilization) failed to adapt to changes and ceased to exist.

However, despite the fact that the very term "civilization" originally referred just to the linear historical separation of social evolution stages (from Latin *civilis* – "civil", "belonging to a state", i.e. civilization means bringing into a condition "appropriate to a citizen"), using it in the other context is more justified.

Any universal model for solving the problems of public administration will only have a chance to succeed if it is implemented in the context of the relevant political, economic, social and ethical culture, because there is no universal idea with respect to an individual's rights and social status and the configuration of power relations. Of course, personnel skills, geographic conditions and a number of other factors are important as well. But the set of conditions making up a civilization in its horizontal rather than vertical dimension is of primary significance.

Civilization means a major integral socio-cultural system including a set of political, economic, spiritual and social subsystems, based primarily on the religious and cultural heritage of a human community.

American political scientist Samuel Huntington, the author of the "clash of civilizations" theory, is the best-known researcher using the civilizational approach. The scholar's principal statement is that a conflict among civilizations correlating with various cultures will play an ever-increasing role in the world in the future.[11]

Huntington identifies nine civilizations:

1   Western civilization;
2   Orthodox civilization;
3   Islamic civilization;
4   Hindu civilization;
5   Sinic, or Confucian, civilization;
6   Japanese civilization;
7   Latin American civilization;
8   African civilization;
9   Buddhist civilization.

The very style of labeling most civilizations makes it clear that Huntington refers not merely to culture but to religious and cultural heritage. In most cases, models of government can also be differentiated according to these groups of states. For this purpose, it is necessary to study the genesis of the social and political institutions characteristic of countries belonging to different civilizations.

> **Genesis** (from a Greek word meaning "to give birth") means beginning, inception or origin.

Questions for self-study:

1 Please distribute the UN member states according to their civilizational affiliation, as per Huntington's theory.
2 What are the differences between the civilizational theories of Toynbee and Huntington?
3 Please give examples of systematic influence of the religious and cultural heritage on political culture in the US, Saudi Arabia and Greece.

Additional materials:

Alekseyeva, T.A. Strategic Culture: Evolution of the Concept – Polis. *Political Studies*. 2012. Vol. 5. pp. 130–147

Huntington, S.P. *The Third Wave: Democratization in the Late 20th Century (Volume 4) the Julian J. Rothbaum Distinguished Lecture Series*. University of Oklahoma Press. 1993

Huntington, S.P. *The Clash of Civilizations and the Remaking of World Order*. Simon & Schuster. 2011

Toynbee, A.J. *Civilisation at Trial. The World and the West*. World Publishing Company. 1968

Notes

1 M. Weber. The Three Types of Legitimate Rule. *Berkeley Publications in Society and Institutions*. 1958. Vol. 4, No. 1
2 C. Geertz. *The Interpretation of Cultures*. Basic Books; 3 edition. 2017
3 L. Guiso, P. Sapienza and L. Zingales. Does Culture Affect Economic Outcomes? *Journal of Economic Perspectives, American Economic Association*. 2006. Vol. 20 (2). pp. 23–48. Spring
4 G.A. Almond and S. Verba. *The Civic Culture: Political Attitudes and Democracy in Five Nations*. SAGE Publications. 1989
5 F.A. von Hayek, D. Antiseri and L. Infantino. *Conoscenza, competizione e libertà* (Italiano). Rubbettino; 1 edition. 1998
6 E. Durkheim. *Moral Education: A Study in the Theory and Application of the Sociology of Education*. Literary Licensing, LLC. 2011

7 F. Nietzsche. *The Will to Power.* Courier Dover Publications. 2019
8 A. Toynbee. *A Study of History.* Oxford: Oxford University Press; 1 edition. 1947
9 P.A. Sorokin. *On the Practice of Sociology* (Heritage of Sociology Series). Chicago: University of Chicago Press; 1 edition. 1998
10 Karl Jaspers. *The Origin and Goal of History* (Routledge Revivals). Routledge. 2014
11 S.P. Huntington. *The Clash of Civilizations and the Remaking of World Order.* Simon & Schuster. 2011

2 Models of public administration

2.1 The Western model of public administration

Western civilization is made up of a group of countries of Catholic and Protestant religious and cultural affiliation situated in Europe, North America and Oceania. It should also be noted that the allocation of the Latin American countries into a separate civilization by Huntington was undoubtedly justified for socio-economic and political reasons, but, from the global perspective, the religious and cultural heritage of the region is based on Catholicism with the addition of some local traditions and peculiarities. Modern states and political institutions in the Latin American countries developed much later in comparison to the Western nations and in a different geographic and socio-economic environment, but Catholic religious and cultural commonality constitutes the root and basis of their statehood. Nevertheless, since there is no confessional difference, but the socio-economic conditions of development differ significantly, the states of Ibero-American civilization could notionally be included in Western civilization as a subgroup that recognizes the political values, institutions and structural models of the Western world, but retains different economic systems.

There are a few essential reasons for which we should start the study of public administration systems in the contemporary world with the Western model.

First, of the top 50 countries in the Human Development Index, only 14 are non-Western. The HDI, a consolidated statistical index reflecting life expectancy, education level and per capita income, is, without a doubt, heavily influenced by the system of government which regulates and secures growth in the said areas. A very similar pattern can be seen in all other global ratings and indices. The average per capita GDP (PPP) in Western countries is $47,493, or almost three times higher than the global average. The same indicator for the countries of Ibero-American civilization is $14,720, or $3,000 below the world level. However, this group includes countries significantly exceeding the global average (Panama – $25,509, Chile – $25,223, Uruguay – $23,531, Argentina – $20,567).

Gross Domestic Product (GDP) (measured according to purchasing power parity (PPP)) per capita is a macroeconomic indicator reflecting the market value of all finished goods and services produced in a country for a given year by the average person, where the exchange rate of any currencies is measured by their purchasing power to be determined with respect to a certain set of goods and services.

Second, it is the Western model of public administration that is seen as a universal configuration of government's relationship with the public and of its internal structure that should be implemented in all parts of the world, without exception. Despite that this approach is not justified, and the sad consequences of some attempts to impose the political systems and institutions of this civilization upon non-Western countries where they are irrelevant are obvious, most elements of public administration in Western countries are still considered a benchmark for the quality and efficiency of systems all over the world.

The diverse forms of government, political-territorial arrangements and government structures in Western countries may give the impression that the public administration systems in those countries have nothing in common except for their democratic nature. In fact, the Western countries, however different in their mechanisms for the formation and implementation of public administration, are similar in their perception of its substance, manner of organization and goal setting.

One could identify the following key institutions of public administration within Western civilization:

- Republicanism;
- Democracy;
- Decentralization of power.

Each of the Western countries will have its own specific institutions developed due to the specific features of their local political culture. But the system of public administration in Western countries will always be based on these principles, without which nobody can imagine a contemporary government in Europe, the US, Australia and the rest.

Before we proceed to a substantive discussion on republicanism, democracy and decentralization, it is necessary to review the reasons why they originated in countries belonging to Western civilization.

The historical existence of the Church as a separate power in Western countries, sometimes above and at other times equal to secular government, with its own doctrine and colossal influence on all social processes, has played a key role in the evolution of those contemporary institutions which ensure the separation of powers, accountability, elections and institutionalization of government.

The accountability of government refers to those conditions of a political system under which government is accountable to its electorate for the exercise of its powers and the performance of its duties, takes into account any critical comments or demands in its activities and is responsible for any failure to perform its duties, incompetence or fraud.

Institutionalization means the perception of government by the public, according to which governmental offices and organizations are seen as abstract entities rather than specific persons.

In this regard, the policy pursued by Hildebrand of Sovana, later elected Pope Gregory VII, was a turning point. He overturned the concept of government-church relations by calling the king just a layman who had no powers in the clerical area that could have made him different from the other people.

In this sense, Gregory VII not only reserved for himself the right to appoint hierarchs but also drew an overall boundary between the Church and the state. Shortly after that, codes of laws describing the powers and regulating the duties of both the Church and government appeared.

Canon law (i.e. the law of the Church) became the first systematized body of law in medieval Europe and later served as a model for the secular legal systems developed subsequently.

This example clearly demonstrates not only the potential of religion for influencing political, legal and social processes but the fact that depending upon this influence resulted in the formation of a government model characterized by separation, accountability, rotation and election in one case and in the formation of a totally different political system in another case.

Initially, Christianity had been a religion of small, secluded communities, and it took 300 years for them to come to a sort of systematized doctrine. And during those 300 years, Christianity was in very strong opposition to government. Taken together, these factors shaped a political culture promoting the occurrence and operation of contemporary Western political institutions, which will be discussed in more detail next.

Republicanism

The republican mechanisms for the exercise of state power are now virtually indispensable when it comes to the need to ensure the democratic nature and efficiency of government. In most cases, even the constitutional monarchies of the Old World, despite the existence of a hereditary head of state, generally prefer to utilize such republican mechanisms as the election and rotation of the executive and the separation of powers among the executive, legislative and judicial branches for the operation of government.

Humankind has known the republic as a form of government since antiquity. It is commonly believed that the term itself was first used 500 years before Christ in Rome, but it is clear that the ancient republic and the contemporary one radically differ from each other.

The ancient republic in Rome reserved power strictly to its aristocracy, the patricians, who controlled the Senate. In a contemporary republic, no class restrictions with respect to the filling of positions in government can apply.

But contemporary republics have other problems as well – first, one should note that they can't be used as universal model for any political system. The attempt to insist, as part of liberal political discourse, that republicanism is a universal tool and must be of a strictly secular nature has failed in the contemporary world. It becomes more and more evident that the institutions of contemporary republicanism operate best in countries sharing the Christian civilizational and cultural heritage.

The ideas of republican democracy do not constitute a stage in a uniform evolution of all of humankind moving in a single direction without any alternative, so that the point achieved by a given country on this way would be measured by its approaching these standards.

In fact, the republic in its current form, and its ideological and theoretical basis, principles, mechanisms and institutions, is the result of evolution of Christian society.

Republic (from Latin *res pubblica*, "common cause") is a form of government in which sovereignty is exercised by the people in accordance with certain statutory procedures, according to the principles of power separation, election and rotation.

In a *presidential republic*, the head of state leads the executive branch, being both the president of the republic and the head of a cabinet, and is elected by the people by way of direct or indirect election, without being responsible to parliament. Cabinet members are appointed directly by the president, who is entitled to remove them.

In the countries of Western civilization, this form of government exists only in the US.

In a *semi-presidential republic*, executive power is exercised by a president, who is elected directly by the people, and by a cabinet that is formed with the participation of parliament. The president is not the head of the cabinet. The person who has won the confidence of parliament leads the cabinet.

The semi-presidential form of government can be exemplified by France, where we can observe a situation of "cohabitation", in which, if the president lacks the parliamentary majority, the actual executive power goes to the leader of the majority in the legislature. However, if the president still possesses the majority, the prime minister is limited to a rather technical role in exercising the powers of the executive.

In addition to France, a semi-presidential (mixed) system also exists in Poland and Portugal.

The *parliamentary republic* is the most common form of government in Western countries. A central role in the state is reserved to its parliament, which, in addition to the exercise of its law-making powers, is also entitled to elect the president of the republic (either alone or jointly with representatives of regional governments), to form a cabinet and to pass a no-confidence vote with respect to the cabinet.

In order to set some limits to the power of parliament, the constitution typically entitles the head of state to dissolve parliament and appoint new elections.

This form of government exists in most European countries, such as Italy, Germany, Austria, Ireland, Slovenia and Croatia.

It should also be noted that even the *constitutional monarchies* of the West, such as the UK, Spain, Belgium and the Netherlands, use very similar mechanisms for government formation. One factual difference is that constitutional monarchies give the role of a president elected for a fixed term to a hereditary monarch, who, nevertheless, is obliged to entrust the leader of the parliamentary majority with the formation of the executive branch.

Democracy

The term "democracy" (from a Greek word meaning "popular rule") has its local analogue in almost all contemporary languages; for example, "*narodovlastiye*" in Russian. But not every popular government is a democracy; hence, when we want to refer to the antique ideal of state order, we typically use the word of Greek origin.

However, both the contemporary republic and democracy have little in common with their counterparts in antiquity. For Enlightenment thinkers and later authors, the desire to demonstrate that political traditions and culture were inherited from the pre-Christian systems of public administration dictated the need to draw parallels with ancient Greece and Rome. But whereas the republic, although in a different form, had already been a real form of government in the Middle Ages, democracy as a political regime and a principle of government became part of political discourse only at the beginning of the 20th century.

Today, democracy is understood as a political regime based on the idea that power in a country should belong to its people, who exercise it either directly or through their representatives. For this purpose, the people include all citizens of the country, subject to certain universal limitations, typically related to age.

Ancient democracies were mostly based on a direct vote principle, but the voters accounted for not more than 10 per cent of the population, whereas up to 90 per cent were slaves who possessed no rights at all.

> **Direct democracy** refers to the ancient form of political regime in which free citizens directly made decisions by voting on specific matters.

In the ancient world, the Greeks often referred to the democratic and, accordingly, free nature of their government in the context of their conflict with the Persians in order to depict the Persian system as tyrannical and, consequently, slavish. Despite the rather skeptical attitude of the greatest ancient Greek philosophers toward democratic rule, which was always under the threat of transforming into ochlocracy (mob rule), it is this form of government that has become associated with the ancient Greek city-states, first of all Athens.

Contemporary democracy is diverse and significantly differs not only from civilization to civilization but also within the Western world itself. The US, France and Italy are all democracies. In the US, however, the population votes not directly for presidential candidates, but for electors, which has repeatedly resulted in differences between the number of supporters of a given candidate and the number of votes cast for him or her. In France, the population elects the head of state directly, and with the support of the parliamentary majority the head of state so elected will be in full control of the executive branch of government in the country. In Italy, since the establishment of the republic in 1947 and until 2000, a cabinet lived for seven to eight months on average, and since 2011, after Silvio Berlusconi had served as prime minister, there were five successive prime ministers for whom the population did not vote in an election. Each of them came into power due to coalition agreements among parliamentary factions, often without participation in an election campaign.

Nevertheless, all of the nations mentioned previously are democracies, since the key attribute of a democracy is not as much the mandatory election of a national government by the population as its accountability to the citizens. The totalitarian regimes in certain European countries in the early 20th century resulted from transparent and fair elections. Moreover, any popular vote in Nazi Germany, Fascist Italy and Franchist Spain would have shown the indisputable leadership of the relevant dictators in public opinion for a long time. But this does not mean that those states could have been called democracies.

The key attribute of democracy is the guaranteed accountability of government to the public. It can and should be secured by very different ways. The republican mechanisms of government operation will eventually promote the accountability of the executive branch by making it dependent upon the legislative branch. Both branches must observe the law; that is, ensured by the activities of the judiciary and the law enforcement system.

Elections are the most obvious option for the public to express its will. Electoral processes are supposed to enable the public to manifest its position with respect to the political programs, ideas and approaches of those forces, which claim access to the distribution of power. But it is increasingly common that elections, including in Western countries, happen to be a personal conflict or show, instead of being a conflict of ideas and political programs, which results in political and government crises and prevents putting together a competent and efficient government system capable of addressing the most pressing issues.

As defined by Joseph Schumpeter, democracy is the institutional arrangement for arriving at political decisions in which individuals (elites) acquire the power to decide, by means of a competitive struggle for the people's vote.[1] But the most universal concept was proposed by Giovanni Sartori, according to whom democracy is the procedure or mechanism that generates open polyarchy (a system of groups competing with each other at elections), assigns power to the people and effectively ensures the accountability of leaders to the people.[2]

That being said, a number of researchers, such as the Italian scholar Luciano Canfora, believe that contemporary European governments are essentially oligarchic regimes operating under the cover of an electoral machine intended to legitimate the power of the elite through the privileged position of the executive and majoritarian electoral mechanisms.[3]

Decentralization

Irrespective of the form of government and political system, most government models in the countries of Western civilization are based on the principle of government decentralization in both vertical and horizontal terms.

It is traditionally believed that government decentralization is about the delimitation of powers between the national and regional authorities – the key test in determining where a given country is a federation or a unitary state. But decentralization is a more complex concept that is not limited to the functional distribution of powers among the various tiers of government.

Like any other institutional arrangements in Western countries, decentralization is based on civilizational principles. The government principles set forth in the key documents of the European Union and the laws of its member states include the principle of subsidiarity, according to which a problem should only be solved at a higher level if its solution at a lower level appears to be impossible.

At the same time, subsidiarity is a principle proposed by the Catholic Church, which has traditionally stated that a central authority should play a "subsidiary" (supportive) rather than "subordinating" (dominating) role by addressing only those tasks which cannot be sorted out at the local level.

A number of Western nations, such as the US, Germany, Austria, Belgium, Canada and Switzerland, are federations. But a vast number of countries commonly believed to be unitary appear to be closer to a federation when it comes to examining the status of their constituent regions and the scope of the regions' actual powers. Such countries include Italy, Spain and Portugal.

These countries have, as a rule, the following specific features:

1 Certain powers are delegated to the regional level through delimitation of competences between the central government and the regions in the constitution and constitutional acts;
2 The regional authorities must be elected;
3 One of the chambers included in the national legislature or a portion of its sole chamber is formed according to a regional principle;
4 Regional entities participate in the activities of central authorities;
5 Parliamentary republics may also provide for the participation of regions in the election of the head of state.

Nevertheless, according to a series of indicators, these states are not federations, since their constitutions do not include a federal political-territorial structure, the constituent parts of those states lack sovereignty and, most importantly, the process of regionalization in those countries is not irreversible, in contrast to federations.

Regionalization is the process aimed at creating an interrelated political and economic system providing a special status for regional entities in the political system of a country, enabling regions to participate in public administration and supporting their relative economic and fiscal independence within a unitary state.

For example, the Constitution of Brazil prohibits any amendments to the Constitution to the extent they are related to the federal structure of the country. A similar rule is contained in the German Constitution, which prohibits any amendments to the fundamental law of the country to the extent they are related to the federal structure of Germany.

But, if we examine the rules concerning the status of regional territorial units in Italy and Spain, it will be clear that no special protection is provided for regionalism in those countries.

Regionalism is an interrelated political and economic system providing a special status for regional entities in the political system of a country, enabling regions to participate in public administration and supporting their relative economic and fiscal independence within a unitary state.

The Constitution of Italy provides that the republican form of government in the country cannot be changed, but if any political force wishes to amend the relevant sections of the Constitution regulating the political-territorial structure of the country, it would be sufficient for it to hold the majority in both chambers of parliament for at least three months.

Concerning the reasons why the decentralized system of government has developed, such factors as the historical existence of certain parts of a country as independent entities in political and geopolitical reality, the fact that the local population identifies itself to a higher degree with the relevant region than with the nation as a whole, and the political, socio-cultural, socio-economic and ethno-geographic differences among the regions comprising a single state are traditionally discussed.

But the widespread practice of using a decentralized government model in Western countries has, however, its civilizational foundations shaped by religious and cultural factors.

In the constitutional documents of the European Union, the tendency for the horizontal and vertical distribution of government powers in member states is described by the term "subsidiarity", derived from the Latin word *"subsidium"*, which means "assistance" or "support". In its current meaning, it stems from the social theory of the Catholic Church – the doctrinal texts discussing the matters of social justice, economics and the place of government in the life of society.

In Catholic doctrine, subsidiarity is intended to solve several problems:

1 The protection of personal freedom and rights;
2 More efficient regional governance;
3 The higher responsibility of the central authority in situations where action is required from it.

In contemporary political philosophy, subsidiarity means that government functions and tasks should be performed at the level as close to the public as possible, whereas a higher tier of government should assume only those powers that cannot be efficiently exercised at the lower level.

But states increasingly tend to prefer a decentralized system of governance on the premise that it could ensure more democracy, because a lower tier of government is closer to the population and any devolution of powers from the center reduces the potential for authoritarian rule or dictatorship. Moreover, decentralization is the preferable form of political-territorial administration in terms of financing and governance efficiency, as reflected in a series of international documents, including the UN Development Program.

This kind of decentralization, where power is delegated from the center to the regions, that is, from a higher level to a lower one, is commonly called *vertical.*

As concerns *horizontal* decentralization, this term is usually used to describe a situation in which none of the branches of government enjoys too much power, each of them has equal access to the mechanism of checks and counterbalances and civic society elements are involved in discussing and drafting government decisions.

The constitutional reservation of certain powers to specific public authorities is not the only possible tool for decentralization. Certain informal rules applicable in a political system often promote the implementation of the power devolution principle. Representative democracies where a direct mandate may be granted to a given politician rarely occur in the Western world.

> **Representative democracy** refers to the exercise of power by the people not directly but through their elected, duly authorized representatives.

In Italy, for example, in order to be elected prime minister, a politician should gain support from one of the political parties that has won enough votes at a parliamentary election, after which it should, as a rule, enter into a coalition with other factions and then be able to convince the legislative body to vote for that politician as its candidate. Thus the prime minister and the entire cabinet are responsible to parliament as a whole, the ruling coalition, their own political party and often a certain faction inside the party.

In the US, despite that the nation is headed by its president, elected through a non-parliamentary procedure, the procedure itself involves a rather time-consuming selection stage. First, a candidate should gain support from one of the two political parties, including both voters and key party sponsors, officials and activists. Then the population will be invited to vote not for the candidate as such, but for electors, who will then determine the winner of the presidential race. Therefore, as in the case of parliamentary Italy and Germany, there exists a *multi-step procedure* securing the decentralization of public authorities with respect to both their formation and operation.

Decentralization reforms were a key element of public administration reform in many EU member states, mostly during the 1980s and 1990s. At the same time, the EU countries tend to reduce the staff of local and regional governments by merging political units or eliminating one of the government tiers in order to split its powers between the higher and the lower tiers. Such reforms are mainly aimed at optimizing government expenditures, eliminating any irregularities and defining more particularly the distribution of responsibility among the administrative tiers.

In most EU member states, there are two or three administrative tiers within the executive branch of government, whereas seven member states have four administrative tiers (Austria, Belgium, Germany, Spain, Italy, Poland and France) and Portugal has five.

For instance, the political-territorial structure of Italy is as follows:

- Country
- Region
- Province
- Municipality

The existence of more than three administrative tiers is usually associated with the largest member states, except for Belgium, where it results from language-based regional differences, and Portugal, where a special status is assigned to the archipelagos known as Madeira and the Azores.

The number and size of local governments may vary significantly as well. For example, France ranks first among all member states in terms of the number of municipalities (35,416), but in terms of population per municipality it is similar to the Czech Republic and Slovakia (1,600–1,800). On the other hand, the Netherlands, the UK and Ireland have the most compact structure of local governments, with more than 150,000 residents per administrative unit on average. The horizontal distribution of power in European countries is as diverse as the vertical one. If we use the number of ministries to measure the scope of powers assigned to the executive, then their number varies from eight in Hungary to 26 in the UK. However, the number of executive authorities in a country in no way correlates to its size. Rather small countries as Denmark, Luxembourg and Croatia have many more of them than Spain, the Netherlands or Germany.

Questions for self-study:

1 What formula is used to calculate the per capita GDP (PPP)?
2 Please distribute the Western countries according to the criteria of their form of government and political-territorial structure.
3 What are the key differences between the Latin American countries and the states of Europe and North America?

Additional literature:

Canfora, L. *Democracy in Europe: A History of an Ideology*. John Wiley & Sons. 2008
Pettit, P. *Republicanism: A Theory of Freedom and Government*. Oxford: Oxford University Press. 1999
Pollitt, C. and G. Bouckaert. *Public Management Reform. A Comparative Analysis – Into the Age of Austerity*. Oxford: Oxford University Press. 2017
Torkunov, A.V. *Along the Road to the Future – 2.5*. Moscow: LKI. 2017

2.2 The Orthodox model of public administration

Orthodoxy is currently the prevailing religious group in Russia, some Balkan countries (Greece, Serbia, Bulgaria, Romania, North Macedonia and Montenegro), Ukraine, Belarus, Moldova, Georgia, Armenia and Cyprus.

With more than 300 million believers, it is the third-largest Christian church after Catholicism (1.25 billion) and Protestantism (800 million).

In Orthodox countries, the average per capita GDP based on purchasing power parity is about $17,000. Given the average global level fluctuating around $18,000, this figure appears to be close to the global average. However, this figure is significantly lower than the figures for the European Union, where the average GDP (PPP) is about $43,000.

The territorial span of Orthodoxy is much narrower than that of the Western Christian denominations. Moreover, the Orthodox religion is in itself less global than Catholicism. The Orthodox churches are closely associated with the relevant nation states and their territories, enjoy broad autonomy and do not recognize the supremacy of any patriarch, except that the Bishop of Constantinople is deemed "the first in honor". Otherwise, those churches are independent and may demonstrate quite different approaches toward certain matters.

It should be noted that during the period when nation states came into existence in Europe, the so-called Peace of Westphalia (1648) was entered into, and the principles of government in the Western countries began to evolve, most countries belonging to the Orthodox civilization had been devoid of their own statehood and subordinate to the Islamic Ottoman Empire for several centuries.

Starting at the end of the 14th century and during the 15th century, the Ottoman Empire had conquered almost the entire territory of Greece, except for the Ionian Islands, Crete and some parts of the Peloponnese that joined it in the 18th century. Having started its armed struggle in 1821, Greece achieved independence from the Ottoman Empire as late as 1832.

The Serbian princes, after their defeat in the Battle of Kosovo, recognized the suzerainty of the Ottoman Empire, and the whole of Serbia was conquered by the Turks in 1459 and remained under Ottoman rule for the next 350 years, until 1878.

Suzerainty is a system of relations characteristic of the feudal era that existed in the form of agreement between the suzerain and the vassal.

Bulgaria lacked independence between the late 14th century and the late 19th century, and the Bulgarian lands were held by the Ottoman Empire, which naturally involved forced conversion to Islam, the displacement of the local population and the destruction of cultural and religious heritage. During that period, the territory of today's North Macedonia was part of Bulgaria.

The territories of Wallachia, Moldavia and Transylvania had become vassals to the Ottoman Empire in 1526 and remained as such until 1877, when the United Principalities of Moldavia and Wallachia declared their independence.

Montenegro had been occupied by the Turks in 1439 and officially become part of the Ottoman Empire in 1499; it remained as such until the Battle of Krusi in 1796, the victory which gave it independence.

The territories of Armenia and Georgia were a field of endless wars between the Ottoman Empire and Persia. After a 40 years' war, the Ottoman Empire and Persia agreed to delimit their respective areas of influence. The eastern Armenian lands were given to the Safavids, and the western ones fell under Ottoman rule. Part of the local population was liberated from the Islamic yoke when the Russian Empire came to Transcaucasia, annexed the territories of the former Erivan, Nakhichevan and Ordubad regions (in 1828) and established the Armenian region. In Georgia, the population was liberated from the Persian and Turkish yoke after the Treaty of Georgievsk was signed and Georgia became part of the Russian Empire in 1783.

The territories of today's Ukraine and Belarus were historically part of the Russian Empire, but some parts of them were also included in Catholic Poland and Lithuania.

Thus, Russia was the only Orthodox country that enjoyed permanent and independent statehood during the period when the leading countries of Europe developed their key concepts of government. That has significantly influenced the political systems of those countries, upon which legal systems, customs and traditions irrelevant to local political culture and representing Islamic civilization were imposed for several centuries.

In the case of Orthodox countries, the role of the Church has been even more important, because it was the Church that had to be responsible for the preservation of ethnic and cultural identity for a number of centuries – the fact that predetermined its strong influence upon social processes in those countries.

In contrast to the Western Christian tradition, primarily the Catholic one, where the pope was historically superior to any monarch and the clerical authorities monitored and supervised the decisions of a secular ruler, the monarch-patriarch relationship followed a somewhat different pattern in the Orthodox tradition.

The Byzantine Empire implemented the "symphony of powers" concept that was described in the epistles of basileuses and patriarchs, theological papers and legal acts.

Basileus was the emperor's title in the Byzantine Empire.

By analogy with human anatomy, the state was also considered a single organism including both the body and the soul. "Since the state, like man, consists of parts, its most important and necessary parts are the monarch and the patriarch; so the peace and welfare of the subjects depend upon the like-mindedness and accord of the monarchical and the patriarchal powers", says the *Isagoge*, a code of laws written in the 9th century.[4]

Whereas the state is perceived in the Western Christian tradition as a phenomenon of secular power existing separately from clerical power that stands above any secular laws, the Orthodox tradition considers it as a combination of both powers.

It should also be noted that, whereas the Church in the Western tradition appears to be a consolidated entity led by one and the same pope who might enter into various relations with the secular leaders of states, but the common cultural tradition remained in place, the picture is somewhat different in the case of Orthodox countries. Correlating to a greater extent with the boundaries of a nation state and with the ethnic factor, the Orthodox Church was more responsive to the impact of any processes which took place within the relevant countries. It was the only organization that was capable of preserving the cultural identity of the local population in those countries, which lived under Ottoman rule, in fact replacing government institutions.

That being said, the Church in the largest and, as one could say, most significant Orthodox country, Russia, was in a totally different position. In 1700, after Patriarch Adrian had died, Peter I prohibited the election of a new patriarch and then established the Clerical Collegium, later renamed the Most Holy Governing Synod. Being a public authority, it managed the Church between 1721 and January 1918. The administrative institutions of the Church were treated as bodies of public administration.

All Orthodox countries are republics, and only Belarus, Russia, Romania and Ukraine are mixed republics in which the president appoints the prime minister with the consent of parliament. The other states follow the parliamentary model of republic in which the parliamentary majority forms the cabinet (Table 2.1).

It should also be noted that Russia is the only federation out of all the Orthodox countries. The other Orthodox countries are officially considered unitary. Moreover, no decentralization of government or delimitation of regional powers is provided for in the majority of them. One exception is Greece, which includes seven decentralized administrations, 13 regions and 325 municipalities enjoying a certain degree of self-government. But even in this case, the decentralized administrations are governed by the general secretary appointed by the government of Greece.

Apparently, the federal structure of today's Russia is inherited from the rule of the Communists, whose policy was focused, among other things, on

Table 2.1 Forms of Government and Political Territorial Structure of Orthodox Countries

Country	Form of Government	Political-Territorial Structure
Armenia	Parliamentary republic	Unitary
Belarus	Mixed	Unitary
Bulgaria	Parliamentary republic	Unitary
Cyprus	Parliamentary republic	Unitary
Georgia	Parliamentary republic	Unitary
Greece	Parliamentary republic	Unitary
Moldova	Parliamentary republic	Unitary
Montenegro	Parliamentary republic	Unitary
North Macedonia	Parliamentary republic	Unitary
Romania	Mixed	Unitary
Russia	Mixed	Federal
Serbia	Parliamentary republic	Unitary
Ukraine	Mixed	Unitary

ethnic segregation and on a system of various ethnic quotas depending not only upon a person's place of birth but also upon his or her ethnic origin.

Indigenization is the Soviet ethnic policy during the 1920s and 1930s aimed at training and promoting to top positions in Soviet republics representatives of local ethnic groups, creating ethnic territorial autonomies, implementing ethnic minorities' languages in official documentation and encouraging the publication of periodicals in local languages.

The Russian Empire, on the contrary, was administered as a unitary state, where nationality was equivalent to ethnic origin, and that determined a rather centralized and uniform system of its territorial governance.

Therefore, most Orthodox countries constitute nation states with a single territory and the parliamentary form of republican government. Russia, with its federal nature and mixed form of government, is an exception.

It should also be noted that one cannot overstate the influence of culture, primarily religious culture, on social processes in Orthodox states. For instance, according to a survey conducted by the US organization Pew Research Center, the highest share of believers among the European countries is in Georgia (99%), Armenia (95%) and Moldova (95%).

What is more important, the survey also indicates that the role of the Church in public life enjoys more support in Orthodox countries than in Catholic ones.

In this regard, more than a third of the population in Orthodox countries is convinced that government should support the propagation of religious values. This list is topped by Armenia (59%), Georgia (52%) and Romania (46%). The lowest results in this regard are shown in Hungary (28%), Croatia (27%) and Poland (25%), where people believe that religion should be separated from politics.

The same organization has conducted a survey regarding the superiority of cultures by asking its respondents the question: "Do you agree that your people are not perfect but your culture is superior to all others?" The top five countries in this regard look as follows:

1   Greece (89%)
2   Georgia (85%)
3   Armenia (84%)
4   Russia (69%)
5   Bulgaria (69%)

On the one hand, Orthodox countries are convinced that their culture is very important and must be preserved and, on the other hand, they believe that it is based on their religious heritage – the fact that predetermines its significance in social and political processes.

It appears rather difficult to make a relatively common timeline for the evolution of government systems in Orthodox countries, because even after the fall of Ottoman rule these countries belonged to different ideological camps and military-political alliances, and that fact also played its role. After World War II, some of the countries (Armenia, Belarus, Russia, Romania, Ukraine etc.) became part of the so-called socialist camp and built a system of government in which Communist Party instrumentalities performed the functions of the executive branch within the framework of a planned economy and eliminated public political competition. During the same period, Greece and Cyprus developed (except for the period of military rule in Athens between 1967 and 1974) in the form of parliamentary republics. Some countries, such as Serbia and Montenegro, were included in Yugoslavia, where the system of government significantly differed from both Soviet and the Western governments. Nevertheless, one can clearly identify a number of specific features typical for the contemporary systems of government in Orthodox states.

Government centralization

As already discussed, almost all Orthodox countries are unitary in terms of their political-territorial structure. This means that regional authorities will be formed by the central ones and be responsible for the implementation of the national policy within their respective territories. In some cases, regions may have their own budgets or even elected heads, but the Orthodox countries most commonly have a straightforward vertical structure of government in which regions are obliged to implement the policy of the national authorities.

On the one hand, most countries of this civilizational affiliation lack any historical pre-requisites for the formation of a decentralized state; on the other hand, there are no civilizational reasons for such an arrangement. Most Orthodox states are monoethnic and do not experience any difficulties associated with the need to represent the interests of ethnic minorities concentrated in a given area. From a geographic perspective, most of them are also rather small and compact countries, without any extremely distant territories.

At the same time, Orthodox countries have no tradition similar to subsidiarity in Western civilization. Perhaps a different church structure is one of the reasons. Whereas Catholicism grew as a supra-national and universal union, for which it was necessary to ensure self-governance in various parts of the world, Orthodoxy was always linked to a specific ethnic group, and then to a specific state. Largely because of this, any forms of integration or consolidation are often more feasible for Western states than for Orthodox ones, taking into consideration the almost uniform civilizational and cultural tradition of the former.

Russia is an exception to these rules. Its size and structural features could allow one to call it at least a sort of "subcivilization", if not a separate civilization. Being a multi-ethnic country that includes locally concentrated groups belonging to all global religions, it still remains an Orthodox state, since the Russian language and culture are the only link connecting all of the peoples and ethnic groups residing in its territory.

Although formally a federation, it is also distinguished by centralization of its government. In the vertical dimension, despite the delimitation of competences between the federation and its constituent regions (subjects), the regions are unequal in terms of the level of their socio-economic development and, as a result, any model of their fully self-supporting existence is clearly unfeasible. Out of the 85 subjects constituting the Russian Federation, only Tatarstan; Moscow; St. Petersburg; the Leningrad, Moscow, Samara, Sakhalin, Sverdlovsk and Tyumen regions; and the Nenets,

Khanty-Mansi and Yamal-Nenets autonomous districts do not receive federal grants. The other 73 regions depend upon so-called equalization grants.

> **Grant** means a budget appropriation intended to cover any anticipated losses or to balance any lower-level budgets.

Horizontal centralization takes a special shape in Russia as well. Because of it, the institution of the head of state plays the key role in the country. Despite the activities of all institutions required for a mixed republic, such as parliament, the cabinet and the judiciary, the scope of decisions being made by the president exceeds the respective figures in Western states by several times.

During the period between 2012 and 2018, for instance, the president of Russia signed 4,522 decrees.[5] In the US, a similar legal act is called an "Executive Order". For the same period, the head of state in the US issued 259 executive orders.[6] The 17-fold difference demonstrates not only the different roles of the president in Russia and the US, but also a rather notional nature of the republican government models, according to which Russia is a mixed republic and the US is a presidential republic. The American system, although containing no mechanism for the participation of the legislative branch of government in the formation of the cabinet, provides for an extremely important role for Congress, which enjoys broad powers, so that it is often capable of restricting the head of state in the exercise of his or her functions. In Russia, however, despite the mixed republican model established in its Constitution, the system of public administration emphasizes the central role of the head of state, who often exercises hands-on control in the most complex or crisis-ridden sectors of the country.

Bureaucracy

The countries of the Orthodox civilization have political and party systems whose contents are quite different. Greece, after its military rule had ended, developed a two-party system with the right-wing and the left-wing parties alternating in power. The marginal party SYRIZA, whose cabinet, however, survived for less than four years, temporarily broke this tradition. In Bulgaria, diverse political forces have participated in cabinet formation since the 1990s, so its system can be called a multi-party one. In a number of Orthodox countries within the post-Soviet space, a change of power has only been possible through anti-constitutional acts, such as civil disorder leading to a coup d'état. Russia has developed a ruling-party system in which the ruling party associated with the head of state controls more political resources than do the other forces, despite that the latter are free to operate and act.

Such differences should have resulted in radically divergent models of government, including the patterns of bureaucracy. However, despite the different configurations of opportunities to gain political power, Orthodox countries are similar in terms of the tools for its direct exercise.

Being heirs to the Byzantine Empire, the Orthodox countries have inherited a rich tradition of somewhat unique bureaucracy arrangements. Being in public service was in itself deemed the greatest achievement for people in any social class. Business life in Constantinople was represented by simple commercial production that provided craftspeople and traders with very modest means of subsistence. But those who were lucky to increase their income in some way preferred to spend it for the purchase of a title or office.

Bureaucracy played not only administrative but also political and social roles, since the existence of a numerous staff of public servants made the residents of the empire believe that the country was stable. The complicated, multi-level and ramified system of bureaucracy sent all key matters for decision to the palace of the emperor, whose favor was a better measure of an official's career success than his position and rank. The complexity of the structure, system of relations and organization inherent in the bureaucracy eventually led to the enhanced centralization of government, in which the emperor was the only capable decision-maker.

In current conditions, Orthodox countries often pay attention to the need to cut their bureaucracy to a significant extent. But, as demonstrated by various statistical data, there is no considerable excess in the number of public servants in Orthodox countries in comparison to the global average. The Heritage Foundation issues its annual index of economic freedom in the world, which includes as one of its components the GDP percentage being spent for bureaucracy. The average figures for Orthodox countries are consistent with the global level, 37.1 per cent against 31.9 per cent (Table 2.2).

The methods for counting public servants are often questioned. First, an accurate comparison among different countries seems to be impossible, because this term generally covers different groups of people. In Russia, public servants include only those persons who belong to public civil service. In most European countries, this also includes any persons involved in the performance of public work. Second, statistical inaccuracies resulting in big but false conclusions can arise even in the same state over a certain period of its evolution.

For instance, they often say that the number of public servants was lower in the Soviet Union than in contemporary Russia. But such calculations ignore the fact that party and non-governmental organizations integrated

Table 2.2 Bureaucracy Spending in Countries Belonging to Orthodox Civilization

#	Country	Percentage
1	Armenia	26.4
2	Belarus	44.2
3	Bulgaria	34.7
6	Greece	50.6
5	Georgia	29.6
4	Cyprus	38.7
7	North Macedonia	31.6
8	Moldova	36.9
10	Russia	35.4
9	Romania	32.1
11	Serbia	42.8
12	Ukraine	42.1
	Average	**37.1**
	World	33.9

with the government mechanisms often performed some of the functions that are currently performed by the executive branch of government.

Moreover, a comparative study based on the commonly used criterion of the number of public servants per 100 persons would appear to be inappropriate even within the limits of today's Russia, since one should also take into account the size of the various regions, their geographic patterns and their social conditions.

Therefore, concerning the specific features of bureaucracy in Orthodox countries, it is not the number of public servants but the organization of their activities that matters. Despite the ever-increasing use of technologies associated with New Public Management and Public Governance, many operational aspects of the executive remain unchanged.

An excessive number of regulations, the permission-based rather than notification-based mode in which most supervisory authorities operate, as well as other problems with respect to bureaucracy organization still remain the center of attention for both the leadership and the public.

That being said, we also know of examples where project-based and digital approaches in the field of public service have been successfully implemented. Russia, in particular, has established one-stop shops, so-called multifunctional centers, which have eliminated the need to visit several different departments in order to obtain documents required for a certain certificate. All that is required from an individual is to apply to one of the centers that runs a comprehensive database, making it possible to obtain any necessary information within a short time.

The multifunctional center for the provision of public and municipal services arranges for the provision of public and municipal services on a "single-window" basis in accordance with the cooperation agreements entered into with federal executive authorities, the authorities in charge of the state non-budgetary funds, the executive authorities of the relevant Russian regions and local governments.

The multifunctional center operates in a manner that eliminates any contact between the applicant and any employees of the authorities directly providing such public or municipal services; the employees of the multifunctional center itself are the only points of contact.

The multifunctional center can also arrange for the provision of:

1   Any services that are necessary or mandatory for the provision of public or municipal services;
2   Any services that are offered by any public or municipal institutions or other organizations that deal with a state assignment/order or a municipal assignment/order;
3   Any additional/related services (notarial services, banking services, copying/reproduction services, local or intra-zone public-use communication services as well as free access to legal reference systems);
4   Any services associated with the reception of applications for the selection or replacement of a health insurance company, the forwarding of such applications and any documents attached thereto to the relevant health insurance companies and the delivery of any mandatory health insurance policies or temporary certificates issued by such health insurance companies (pursuant to the contracts entered into by the multifunctional center with such health insurance companies);
5   Any services offered by the joint stock company "Federal Corporation for the Development of Small and Medium-Sized Enterprises" to small- and medium-sized businesses, including the use of the unified portal of public and municipal services, regional portals of public and municipal services and any other IT tools created for the online provision of public and municipal services;
6   Any services for legal entities and individual entrepreneurs associated with the provision of public and municipal services required in order to start and develop business activities;
7   Any services associated with the reception of applications for inclusion in the list of voters or referendum participants with respect to the election of the president of the Russian Federation, the election of state authorities in any Russian region or a referendum in any Russian region

in accordance with the procedure for the inclusion of local residents in the list of voters or referendum participants, as approved by the Central Election Commission of the Russian Federation.

Another nice example is the digitalization of public administration that is more developed in certain sectors of Russian bureaucracy than in some advanced Western states. For instance, the option to complete applications and obtain the necessary documents and permissions through online resources not only reduces the time that an individual spends on bureaucratic procedures but is also an important tool to eliminate factors encouraging corruption.

In this area, Russia's top priorities are:

1   The digitalization of public administration;
2   Online interdepartmental interaction;
3   The implementation of paper-free document circulation at state authorities;
4   IT and telecommunications infrastructure for state authorities;
5   The implementation of Russian-made software at state authorities;
6   The development of public infrastructure for cloud computing;
7   Open data.

Since 2015, Russia has been supporting a functionality with which individuals can receive electronic information instead of hard-copy letters without losing the legal status of such information.

It is prohibited for state authorities and local governments to request from individuals and legal entities any documents or information that are in possession of other state authorities or local governments (except for documents in personal storage). About 400 public services are offered as part of interdepartmental information cooperation.

Since 2016, a similar prohibition has been applied to state monitoring/supervisory bodies for the purpose of their inspections. Such state monitoring/supervisory bodies are not entitled to request from legal entities and entrepreneurs 188 types of documents (for example, an excerpt from the Unified State Property Register with respect to any property; information from the Unified State Taxpayers Register; information on the amount (or the absence) of any debt for taxes, charges, penalties or fines for violations of law). These and some other documents should be requested electronically with the use of the Unified Interdepartmental Electronic Interaction System.

Electronic interaction among state authorities with respect to any state or municipal service is supported by the Unified Interdepartmental Electronic

Interaction System (UIEIS). In 2017, the total number of transactions (requests and replies) in the system was 20.2 billion.

Questions for self-study:

1 Please compare the concept of secular/clerical power separation in the Catholic and the Orthodox Churches. How do they correlate with the forms of government in the countries of the Western and the Orthodox civilizations, respectively?
2 Please compare the scope of central government powers in the various countries of Orthodox civilization.
3 Please discuss the key aspects of Public Governance digitalization in the Russian Federation.

Additional materials:

Harris, J. *The Lost World of Byzantium*. New Haven and London: Yale University Press. 2015
Kuz'bozhev, E.N. and I.A. Koz'eva. *The History of Public Administration in Russia*. Moscow: YURAIT. 2015
Nisnevich, Y.A., A.V. Malashenko and A.V. Ryabov. *The Rise of a Post-Industrial Civilization: From Digitalisation to Barbarism*. Moscow: YURAIT. 2019

2.3 The Islamic model of public administration

According to various estimates, there are more than 1.8 billion Muslims in today's world. They prevail in 49 countries, being the youngest and fastest-growing group of believers among the officially recognized monotheistic religions.

The average per capita GDP (PPP) across Islamic civilization is $17,201. As compared to the global average of $17,914, this figure may appear a rather agreeable one, without any significant abnormality. However, the development gap among the various countries of Islamic civilization is not just large, it is tremendous. If we delete from the list six states that are extremely rich in resources but not very populated (Qatar – $129,360, Brunei – $71,759, Kuwait – $71,020, UAE – $69,222, Saudi Arabia – $55,730, Oman – $47,933), and the figure drops to $9,062, that is, two times lower than the global average and almost five times lower than the average figure for Europe.

Another important feature allowing one to sort the Islamic countries into groups is their affiliation with various denominations within Islam. The main branches of Islam are known to be Sunni and Shia. Of course, there also exist numerous subdivisions within these branches, as well as other sects, such as the Ismailites and the Alawites. The latter, however, do not account for the majority in any countries of the world, and even in those countries where they form a numerous minority, they are nevertheless more inclined either to Sunni or Shia.

In order to understand the specific structure of public administration in Islamic countries, one needs to trace the history of formation and evolution of political philosophy and doctrine in both Islam as a whole and in its two main branches.

Whereas Christianity initially came into existence as a religion opposing the government of the country where it was propagating (the Roman Empire) and later continued to act in the same manner for more than 300 years, Islam offered its support to state power from the very beginning, being inseparably tied to the idea of a caliphate. Whereas early Christianity was a religion of small groups, Islam was an integral community since its inception.

Despite the fact that Christianity suggests the unimportance of ethnic origin and states that there is "neither Jew nor Greek", it was, at its core, shaped by three cultures: Greek, Roman and Hebrew, and then evolved in accordance with the customs and traditions of those peoples who had adopted it. Particularly in the case of Orthodox countries, Christianity acquired a national aspect, and clerical structures often replaced public institutions when the latter failed.

Islam, on the contrary, ignores nation states and focuses on the concept of *ummah* (community) that does not know any borders, nationalities or ethnic groups. The concept of state called caliphate is widespread in Islam, but it suggests that there must be only one caliphate and that the caliph must perform both secular and religious functions.

Islam was split into two denominations because of a dispute over the legacy of the Prophet Muhammad that had arisen after his death. The key differences between Sunni and Shia lie in the field of law application rather than dogma.

The Sunnis believe that the lawful successors to Muhammad were the first four caliphs – Abu Bakr, Umar, Usman and Ali – and also recognize the numerous traditional stories (*Sunna*) about the Prophet Muhammad and support the leading role of the Muslim community in solving key problems.

The Shiites, on the other hand, believe that, after Muhammad's death, the community should have been ruled solely by his descendants, the children of Fatima, Mohammad's daughter, and Ali, his cousin.

Out of the almost two-billion-strong Muslim population of the earth, Sunnis account for 85 per cent and Shiites for 15 per cent.

Despite the differences occurring within the Muslim world that have arisen both for denominational reasons and for geographic, ethnic or socio-economic ones, there also exists a common system of values and traditions inherent in the political culture of Muslim states.

Out of the seven contemporary absolute monarchies, five represent Islamic civilization. Qatar, the United Arab Emirates, Saudi Arabia, the Sultanate of Brunei and the Sultanate of Oman are states where the form of government is very close to an absolute monarchy. Since the very concept of absolutism has been formed around the historical models of European states, its application to Middle Eastern or African countries is rather notional. However, if we choose between the constitutional and the absolute monarchy, these states would undoubtedly fall under the second category.

Moreover, if we add to their number Bahrain, Jordan, Kuwait and Morocco, which are officially deemed constitutional monarchies but which in fact are significantly different from their traditional European counterparts, it will be obvious that the Islamic states of the Middle East show a sufficient tendency for monarchical rule.

Iran, the main Shiite state, is a theocratic republic formally featuring such institutions as parliament, president and judiciary, but all power is concentrated in the hands of its clerical leader, the *ayatollah*.

Virtually all of the other countries of Islamic civilization are characterized by the dichotomy between the military and religious fundamentalists.

Dichotomy means division into two non-overlapping parts.

That is, wherever there formally exists a republic, power belongs either to military leaders who could be classified, according to Western standards, as authoritarian rulers, but who ensure a relatively secular nature of government and a strong vertical orientation of power, or religious fundamentalists who introduce Sharia rules of law and other specific elements that do not fit into the traditional Western concepts of democratic government.

Fundamentalism refers to any ideological or religious movements that proclaim commitment to the original ideological forms, traditions and values of a certain doctrine and demand to terminate any deviations arising in the course of its evolution and to restore the original purity.

Within the framework of Islam, the functioning of Western political institutions that now are viewed as universal is very difficult to achieve due to
the radically different political culture shaped by the different contents of
its religious doctrine. In Islam, for instance, a Western-style separation of
powers did not emerge historically because both the ideological contents
of its religious doctrine and the role of its religious organization in political
processes were quite different.

A number of very specific principles make the organization of social
institutions in a Muslim society essentially different from that in a Christian one. Islam rules out any possible existence of different Muslim states
as such. "If an oath is given to two caliphs, then kill the second of them",[7]
so that only one ruler can exist for the Muslims. And no one is allowed to
divide the *ummah* (the community of believers) over anything: "if anyone
seeks to destroy your unity and divide you at a time when your power is in
the hands of a single man, whoever he is, kill him".[8] If we add to this that
Islam does not recognize the separation of religious and secular functions,
thus cementing the undivided nature of religious and secular authority, of
religion, politics and government, then it will be clear that the Islamic state
represents a totally different configuration of relations.

Islam has originally been systematized and proclaims a united caliphate,
with a single ruler and unified rules of law, as its goal. Some Islam experts
go still further by stating that, whereas Christianity might be torn apart by
contradictions mainly because of theological matters, the greatest schism in
Islam was caused by caliphate-related issues.[9] The conflict between clerical and secular authority, typical for Christianity, is virtually unfeasible
within the framework of Islam, because one and the same person, that is,
the caliph, represents both kinds of authority. Beginning from the Umayyad
and Abbasid dynasties, "caliph" was the hereditary title of a ruler enjoying unlimited clerical and secular authority. One exception to that was the
Mamluk Sultanate, where the caliphs retained solely their clerical authority
but secular authority belonged to the sultans. However, this practice did not
last long, and the Ottoman sultan Selim I destroyed the Mamluk state and
immediately assumed the title of caliph, possessed by subsequent sultans
until 1924.

There also exists the opinion that Islam has been focused on creating a
society rather than a state, since it has no vertical hierarchy. While agreeing
with this position, I must note that Islam simply leaves no room for nation
states as such. That is, one cannot say that Islam seeks to create a society
without government or existing across nation states. Its ultimate goal is a
single caliphate led by one caliph.[10] Islam does not envisage the existence of
nationalities, ethnic groups and, accordingly, nation states. Humankind as a

whole must be a single *ummah* under both secular and clerical (a distinction fundamentally alien to Islam) leadership of a caliph.

Initially, the principal enemy of Islam on its way toward domination in the Arab world was tribalism – the aspiration of a social group for cultural and socio-political segregation based on clan or tribal factors. Muhammad's teaching was intentionally directed against tribes, because it proclaimed the existence of a single *ummah* (community) loyal to Allah rather than to any tribe. That position was important for creating the basis for future transformation, but Arab tribal fragmentation continued to play a prominent role in the political structure of Muslim countries.

In the Islamic world, a unique model of "military slavery" was used in an attempt to defeat tribalism. It was invented by the Abbasid dynasty in the middle of the 9th century as a tool to overcome the persistent weaknesses of tribal units as the basis for the Muslim military forces. Since power had been concentrated in the hands of a *wazir*, government centralization sharply increased. The Abbasids suggested that military slavery could be a method for mitigating the unpredictable nature of a political authority based on family ties. Caliph Al-Mahdi (A.D. 775–785) preferred to appoint slaves rather than relatives to official positions.

This practice reached its peak after the invasion of Central Asia, when the recruitment of local Turks as servicemen began. The slaves did not know their biological parents – they knew only their master and were very loyal to him alone. That was intended to eliminate the problem of nepotism and of conflicting loyal tribes that had been quite common in the traditional Arab society.

Nevertheless, such phenomena as nepotism and tribalism still remain a common trouble for public administration systems in Islamic countries. Being artificially fitted into the constitutional framework of Western-style republics, many Islamic states encounter, in the best case, the imitation of activities by their public and political institutions or, in the worst case, the absolute incapacity of their governments.

Forms of government and Islam

Out of the 49 states belonging to Islamic civilization, ten are monarchies, either absolute or constitutional. However, this designation and subclassification of government forms in Islamic states is rather notional, since it implies analogies to European monarchies. But the system of government in the Muslim world is structured in a somewhat different way.

One example of absolute monarchy is the Sultanate of Brunei, where its sultan is both the head of state and the head of the cabinet. He is also the minister of defense and, more importantly, the religious leader of the country's Muslims. The cabinet he leads consists, for the most part, of his blood relatives.

In another absolute monarchy, Oman, its sultan serves, concurrently, as prime minister, minister of defense, minister of finance, foreign minister and chairman of the Central Bank. Any political parties are banned in the country.

In Saudi Arabia and Qatar, the monarch appoints the members of all councils and assemblies involved in discussing any bills or resolutions. Any activity that is generally assumed part of civic society in Western countries is strictly prohibited here. Law directly bans any political parties, trade unions, protests or meetings.

A unique form of governance is adopted in the United Arab Emirates, which formally constitutes a republican federation of seven absolute monarchies, in which the emir of Abu Dhabi – a hereditary ruler – is elected as president by default.

Such constitutional monarchies as Bahrain or Jordan have formally adopted certain political institutions characteristic of the Western model – two-chamber parliaments, a cabinet accountable to the legislative authority and so on. However, due to the radically different political culture and system of values, these countries have neither political parties nor political ideologies, and the only ideological and theoretical basis for their political and legal development is Islam.

One could give dozens of additional examples, such as Malaysia, a country consisting of 13 states, nine of which are absolute monarchies electing a king, who then appoints governors to the remaining four states. But it is obvious that, irrespective of the specific form in which a monarchical rule is implemented, due to the fundamentally different patterns of their historical evolution, political culture and social stratification, the countries of Islamic civilization have developed hereditary regimes significantly different from the Western model.

But whereas monarchies may be viewed as a relatively habitual and traditional model for the population in Islamic countries, the republic cannot be considered as such and, in the case of Muslim states, assumes very different forms of organization and implementation of government powers.

Most republics in Arab countries emerged following their independence from colonial regimes. The concept of "nation state", however, is hardly applicable to those countries, because virtually none of them represents a relatively homogenous ethno-confessional group. At best, one could speak of a certain majority represented by Sunni Arabs, but it is not sufficient, in terms of numbers, to form a core for the system of government. As a rule, each of the Arab republics in the Middle East has a significant group of

Shiites, Alawites or (similar to them in their views) Kurds, who may belong to the same denomination but are ethnically segregated, Armenians, who represent Christianity, as well as some indigenous local Christian groups who lived there before the Arab conquest (Maronites, Copts, etc.).

Ethno-confessional differences in the region have repeatedly resulted in full-scale hostilities, civil wars or tensions, and this fact has been reflected in the systems of public administration in the relevant states.

Lebanon's model of government was created in 1943, after the country had become independent from France, and is entirely based on the confessional principle of power distribution. For instance, the Constitution of Lebanon provides that the president of the country must always be a Maronite Christian, the prime minister a Sunni Muslim and the speaker of the parliament a Shia Muslim, and the cabinet must include Christians and Muslims in equal numbers. And the parliament – the Assembly of Representatives – must include 64 Muslims (27 Sunnis, 27 Shiites, eight Druzes and two Alawites) and 64 Christians (32 Maronites, 20 Armenians belonging to the Armenian Apostolic Church, two Catholic Armenians, eight Eastern Orthodox Christians, one Catholic Greek and one Protestant).

In Iraq, after the removal of Saddam Hussein from power, the drafting of a constitution was started in August 2003 after the formation of the Iraqi Governing Council, which set up a Constitutional Committee including 12 Shia Arabs, five Sunni Arabs, five Sunni Kurds, one Turkmen and one Assyrian (Christian).

There is growing support for the idea to use an ethno-confessional model of power distribution in order to overcome the effects of the civil war in Syria, whose territory is shared by the Sunni Arabs, Alawites, Kurds, Armenians and Greeks.

A similar picture is typical for most countries in the Middle East, where state borders were in fact determined by the former colonial nations. Because of perennial wars, including both wars among states and civil wars, the toppling of military dictators and the rise of religious fundamentalists to power, the region has lost almost all of its Christian population over the recent decades. It should be noted that the Christians were an indigenous population preceding the Arab conquests and Islamization rather than immigrants or outsiders in those states. Some cities in Syria, Lebanon, Iraq and other countries of the Middle East are among the cradles of Christianity and have colossal importance to that religion.

Other trends are observed in the Turkic republics belonging to Islamic civilization. Being represented principally by the post-Soviet countries of Central Asia and Azerbaijan, as well as Turkey, this group of states tends to adopt forms of government involving a central role of the head of state. In post-Soviet countries, this trend surfaced just after the breakdown of the

Soviet Union, when many of the republics had first achieved their independent statehood. The presidents of those states acquired the status of the nation's founding fathers.

For instance, Article 91 of Kazakhstan's Constitution states that the fundamental principles of the Republic "were established by the Founder of independent Kazakhstan, the First President of the Republic of Kazakhstan – Elbasy", and that his status is not subject to change. This status is, in particular, reflected in a special constitutional law reading, "the First President of the Republic of Kazakhstan, who was the creator of Kazakh independence and who has made an outstanding contribution to the development of sovereign Kazakhstan as a democratic, secular, rule-of-law and welfare state, is the Elbasy. The First President of the Republic of Kazakhstan – Elbasy shall possess, *ex officio*, the title 'Халық каһарманы' (Popular Hero) and a mark of special honour, the Golden Star and the Order of Otan".

Geidar Aliev, the former Azerbaijani president and father of the current head of state, enjoys a special status as well. The Institute of History of Azerbaijan's Academy of Sciences includes a department of "Aliev studies" (*əliyevşünaslıq* in Azeri) that was set up on April 2, 2008; public buildings, mosques, oil tankers, streets and institutions are named after the ex-president.

In Turkmenistan, the second president possesses the official title "Arkadag", which the Turkmen state-owned mass media translate as "stronghold, support and hope", as well as "patron". Gurbanguly Berdimuhamedow, like his predecessor Saparmurat Niyazov, has a lot of unofficial titles, such as "The Leader of the Nation", "The Elite of the Nation", "Merciful Arkadag", "Much-Respected President", "The Glorious Son of His People", "Savior" and "The Honored Elder of the People".

Turkey, as already mentioned earlier, is undergoing the process of Islamization accompanied by the transition from a parliamentary republic to the vertical rule of its president who, in his speeches, increasingly refers to the ideals of the Ottoman Empire and the sultanate.

Islamic countries in Africa often develop hybrid forms of government relying upon both Muslim concepts regarding the role of the head of state, an indivisible *ummah* and the unity of power and the traditions of autocracy and personification (rather than institutionalization) of power that are common to those countries.

Organization of state bureaucracy

In the majority of the aforementioned countries, the public sector is the key employer, because it offers stable jobs on more favorable terms and conditions than the private sector does and is often the only option for employment. Taking into account the rich traditions of bureaucracy in the historical Islamic states, employment in the public sector is highly prestigious, and this fact, against the background of widespread nepotism and patronage, always limits any cuts in the number of public servants and bureaucracy reforms.

Governments typically prefer to follow a traditional step-by-step approach toward budgeting, since in order to maintain political stability it is required to preserve the client-patron structure, which depends upon budgeting processes that ensure benefits for certain social groups.

In a number of countries, centralized bureaucracy has virtually ceased to exist, so that the state has been thrown back to prehistoric times. The ousting of local dictators and the holding of elections, contrary to the hopes of liberal-minded politicians, have cleared the way for anarchy, where the potential and scope of using violence by the various groups are the only means to legitimize state power. This can be brightly exemplified by Libya, where the entire power structure and all resources have actually been appropriated by non-governmental entities. The state has practically fallen apart under such circumstances. The real power belongs to armed groups and movements outside of the state mechanism.

On the other hand, the UAE carries out a large-scale program of reforms in the field of public administration. This country focuses on the implementation of e-government technologies. Each emirate has its own public service portal, and all of them are integrated into a single federal system. The UAE is one of the leading countries worldwide in the provision of online services.

The key areas of state bureaucracy reform in Islamic countries are currently as follows:

1 To develop an up-to-date model of legislation on public service;
2 To set up a database of public servants;
3 To revise the structure of positions in the public sector;
4 To create workforce planning systems;
5 To create new and more efficient training programs.

Any attempt to reform public service, especially as concerns its optimization, is always a difficult process. Any radical steps leading to significant staff cuts and changes in the working conditions and workloads of the bureaucracy result in its potential resistance, not only to that specific reform but to any transformation as well. The most advanced countries of Islamic civilization have succeeded in this area, and now the remuneration of a public servant in the UAE, Qatar, Kuwait and a number of other countries is linked to his or her efficiency, and meritocratic principles have been implemented with respect to the recruitment and promotion of low- and medium-tier employees. In order to modify staffing plans and increase staff performance, one should inevitably enhance the autonomy and independence of medium-tier public administrators operating at the level of departments or divisions, since excessive centralization in this aspect would result in low flexibility and delayed HR decisions poorly responding to the challenges and tasks at hand.

> **Meritocracy** means a system of government arrangements in which a person's abilities and skills rather than social origin determine whether he or she will belong to the elite.

A number of Middle East and North African countries have set up computerized databases including not only the personal data of public servants but also the list of training programs they have received, their key competencies and their ratings. The use of such a system, on the one hand, makes it possible to evaluate the actual potential of the HR reserve for public administration and, on the other hand, offers a platform providing potential employers with access to such data.

Obviously, it is impossible to plan human resources without the elements mentioned earlier, because such activity cannot be planned without knowledge as to what should be done, how to do it and who is to do it. Competitive mechanisms for the filling of state civil service positions, transparent staff recruitment and a flexible system of work organization are the principal criteria in planning the development of human resources.

Finally, the re-training of human resources employed in the field of public service plays an important role. Many countries of Islamic civilization, especially those in the region of the Persian Gulf, such as Saudi Arabia, the UAE, Bahrain, Qatar and Kuwait, prefer to utilize leading experience from the private sector in the educational process; as a result, they often hire business consultants as instructors or use university education programs originally prepared for the private sector.

That being said, it should be noted that this experience is mainly limited to the most developed countries of Islamic civilization, which are not so numerous. The majority of the countries included in this group need to ensure at least some relative degree of controllability of social processes and stability of public institutions. But the experience of such countries as the UAE, Qatar, Kuwait and Jordan demonstrates that there are no cultural or civilizational obstacles for the countries of this group to implement such innovations in the field of public administration.

Questions for self-study:

1 Please compare the form of government in the Islamic Republic of Iran with that in the Kingdom of Saudi Arabia.
2 Please review the position of Islamic states in international ratings and indices.
3 Please compare the experience of public administration reform in the UAE and Turkey.

Additional materials:

Massey, A. and K. Johnston. *The International Handbook of Public Administration and Governance*. Edward Elgar Publishing. 2015
Samier, E. The Islamic Public Administration Tradition: Historical, Theoretical and Practical Dimensions. *Halduskultuur*. 2017
Yenghibaryan, R.V. *21th Century: An Islamic Challenge*. Moscow: Norma. 2016

2.4 The Eastern models of public administration

A certain number of civilizations, taking into account their mixed nature, mutual influence and the spread of their cultural heritage, can be combined, for our purposes, into an "Eastern world". It constitutes a mix of the Buddhist, Confucian, Hindu and Japanese civilizations. Taking into account that no country in the Eastern world had a population which historically followed one particular religion and that the vast majority of the civilizations were spread throughout the territory of different states, they could conditionally be grouped into a bigger group of "Eastern" civilizations.

The *Buddhist* countries include Bhutan, Cambodia, Laos, Mongolia, Myanmar, Sri Lanka and Thailand. The *Confucian* civilization includes China, Singapore and Taiwan. It can also be expanded to include both Koreas, where the role of Confucianism, the official ideology of the Joseon dynasty during 500 years, from 1392 until 1897, was historically important, as well as Vietnam. The *Hindu* civilization is confined to India, Bhutan and Nepal. It would be difficult to include *Japan* in any particular civilization, since its evolution has been influenced by Chinese, Buddhist and the more ancient Altai culture.

The Confucian model

The Confucian, or Sinic (derived from *Qin*, the first dynasty in Chinese history), civilization is a group of countries whose population share the system of thinking and behavior created by the philosopher Confucius (551–479 B.C.) in ancient China. This civilization is special in that Confucianism cannot be called a religion in the classic sense of the word. It is a secular code of conduct rather than a transcendent doctrine of metaphysics.

Metaphysics is a discipline examining the extrasensory principles and first causes of being.

Nevertheless, in the absence of any official religion similar to the Abrahamic ones, Confucianism has assumed the role of a civilizational core for China and Singapore and significantly influenced the evolution of Korea, Japan and a number of other countries where Buddhism currently prevails.

Abrahamic religion is a common name for Judaism, Christianity and Islam, whose followers consider the biblical patriarch Abraham, who embraced the belief in one God and made a covenant with Him, as an exemplary believer.

The average per capita GDP in China, South Korea, Singapore and Hong Kong is $56,403, which is three times higher than the global average of $17,000. In this regard, it should be noted that Singapore ranks fifth in the world at $101,353; Hong Kong ($64,488) and South Korea ($40,112) also stand high on the global list, and the figures for China hover near $18,210.

One of the key principles in Confucianism is the concept of controllability, suggesting that, in order to control others, one should first learn how to control oneself in accordance with universal order. The personal goodness of a ruler spreads good all over the country. This idea is closely connected with the Taoist concept of *wu wei*: the less a ruler does, the more is done. The sovereign, being a calm center around which his country revolves, allows everything to operate uninterruptedly and avoids interference with individual parts of the whole.

Confucius put forward a revolutionary idea of replacing the nobility of blood with the nobility of goodness. According to his concept, a good, ordinary man who develops his qualities can be a noble person, whereas a shameless son of a sovereign can be a little person. Confucius' disciples were recruited from all classes of the Chinese society. This approach largely determined the views of Confucius on the preferred form of government organization, which, in his case, was focused on active promotion of meritocracy. It involved regular testing, examination and evaluation of public servants. In this regard, any person, irrespective of his origin, was eligible to enter civil service. That resulted in the introduction of a system of imperial examinations in China. The system came into operation in the era of the Sui dynasty (A.D. 581–618) and continuously expanded its coverage after that.

Under the Eastern Zhou dynasty (770–256 B.C.), China saw the formation of fully functional states with permanent armies, which were able to enforce the law all over the country. A bureaucracy was set up in order to collect taxes and enforce laws; the Qin state launched a large-scale modernization of the early Zhou's clan-based social order by reducing the role of military aristocracy and directly conscripting numerous peasants. A land reform took property from landlords and granted land directly to peasant households. As many scholars believe, those changes were aimed not at democratization but, on the contrary, at expanding the role of government and then establishing a dictatorship that neither the aristocracy nor the bourgeoisie would be able to restrain. However, the powerful institutions of centralized government and bureaucracy began to play a highly important role in China and still constitute a characteristic trait of the political evolution of this nation.

The People's Republic of China (PRC) is governed by several public authorities. The All-China Assembly of People's Representatives (the Assembly) exercises supreme power in the country, is entitled to amend the Constitution and principal laws and supervises and forms the key public authorities. The Assembly includes almost 3,000 members, and this fact makes it the largest legislative body in the world. A multi-step election procedure is used: at the local level, citizens vote only for electors, who then select candidates at the provincial level. The majority of seats are allocated to the Communist Party of China, since it, as mentioned in the Constitution, is the leading force in the country.

The Assembly holds its approximately two-week-long plenary session on an annual basis and votes for important legislative acts, and the majority of current legislation is adopted by the Permanent Committee of the All-China Assembly of People's Representatives consisting of about 170 lawmakers.

The president of the PRC acts as head of state and implements any resolutions passed by the Assembly, which elects him. The State Council constitutes the executive branch of government led by the prime minister, who must also be approved by the Assembly.

In general, the Chinese governance is not dependant on elections when there is a need to choose the leaders, as the official position usually underlines the fact that it is considered to be risky for such an ethnically, economically and culturally diverse country. However, the vast majority of Western countries, as well as many Orthodox states, have even more complicated structures, which is never an obstacle for elections. The fact that Chinese leaders are not elected following the ballot system but via a unique recommendation and selection of "the wise and able" might be explained through a bigger different civilizational basis, which has always been concentrated on meritocracy and a system able to pick out the most qualified, rather than the most popular. China could be considered a unique country, one which is formed not on a nation-state model but rather on a civilization-state configuration, which unites different nations with common cultural heritage. Jiang Zemin (the fifth president), Hu Jintao (the sixth president) and Xi Jinping (the seventh and current president) all urged party members to rule the country "by virtue".

The procedure of nomination of president of the PRC is one of the examples of the differences between "election" in the Western and Orthodox world and "selection" in the Confucian world. The president is nominated by the National People's Congress Presidium – a 178-member body of the National People's Congress (NPC), composed of senior officials of the Communist Party of China, the state, non-Communist parties and the All-China Federation of Industry and Commerce, those without party affiliation, heads of central government agencies and people's organizations, leading members of all the 35 delegations to the NPC session including those from Hong Kong, Macao, Taiwan and the People's Liberation Army. The NPC then elects the president from a one-name ballot. The ruling Communist Party of China, in practice, reserves the post of president for its current general secretary, who is nominally elected by the Central Committee, which, in turn, is nominally elected once every five years by the National Congress of the Communist Party of China. In practice, however, the selection process is usually done through consultation with the party's Politburo, which many experts consider to be a self-perpetuating body.

China has implemented several administrative reforms that are basically intended to optimize and modernize its government staff. Government functions have been repeatedly redistributed, public administration and corporate governance have been separated and the departments overseeing the largest enterprises have been eliminated. Much attention has been given to standardization, which creates a uniform framework for the budgeting process.

> **Optimization** means the process of selecting, out of all possible alternatives of resource utilization, the one that would produce the best results, often by maximizing the target function.

> **Modernization** means the updating of a target, bringing it into conformity with new requirements, rules or quality standards.

It is important to mention that China has a very complicated structure of territorial administration. Although "Han" ethnicity makes up more than 80 per cent of the total population of China, its population consists of 56 ethnic groups, which comprise the nation in general. Ethnic minorities, being small in numbers compared to the Han, play a vital role in the political life of the country, as they live compactly in predominately separate territories.

The Communist Party of China has partially gone the same way the Soviet Union did in its national self-determination policy, which led to the establishment of national autonomies and regions. In the 1930s, however, China formulated its particular vision of an abstract idea of national self-determination, specifying that national minorities have the right to create their own national-territorial autonomies inside the country. The Constitution of the PRC has constantly updated the parts concerning national-territorial self-government. The territory causing the biggest number of problems has been Xinjiang, which is often called East Turkestan, as there are many representatives from Central Asia living in the region. The region itself makes up one-sixth of the territory of the entire PRC. The Uighur population comprises 8.3 million people (45 per cent) of Xinjiang and often displays an aggressive attitude toward the official capital, Beijing.

Another Confucian state, Singapore, has been developed in a somewhat different way. Despite its small size –692.7 square kilometers inhabited by almost five million people – Singapore is one of the most developed states in today's world, being extremely attractive for investment. Its system of public administration, built according to meritocratic principles, has become the key factor for this success.

It should be noted that Singapore is not homogenous from an ethnic perspective. But the core group around which its public institutions have been formed is represented by the Chinese, who account for 76 per cent of the local population, along with 13 per cent Malay Muslims and 8 per cent Indians. It is the Chinese, belonging to Confucian civilization, who have established the framework of its state power and assumed the key roles in its government.

However, the ethnic and cultural differences have determined public policy content since then. The People's Association (PA) was established on July 1, 1960, as part of the nation-building program to counter racial and political tensions in Singapore during the 1950s and 1960s and promote closer ties among different ethnic groups. The PA is a statutory board that oversees neighborhood grassroots communities and social organizations.

> **The statutory boards of the Singapore government** are organizations that have been given autonomy to perform an operational function by legal statutes passed as acts in parliament. The statutes define the purpose, rights and powers of the authority. They usually report to one specific ministry.

Singapore has chosen decentralization as one of the means to cope with the challenges of multinational and multi-confessional society. In this case, decentralization is not meant as passing power from the central authority to the lower levels of administration. It is rather a type of outsourcing, when the government decides to pass administrative functions to a civil or private sector in order to make it closer to the people. So, it is quite close to the aforementioned Confucian principle of *wu wei*: the less a ruler does, the more is done.

One example of this is the Community Development Council – a government-led program to organize grassroots organizations and community programs into smaller, local units as a bridge between the government and the community. It encourages volunteerism from the wider community and organizes community and social assistance programs with the help of a monetary grant from the government.

An autonomous entity within Malaysia since 1963 and an independent state since 1965, Singapore inherited the British colonial tradition of public administration. It established a system of parliamentary rule centered on the People's Action Party (PAP), which has been governing the country since 1959 by means of its absolute majority of more than 90 per cent.

The executive in the country is represented by its president, who is elected by direct vote of its citizens for a term of six years, is a ceremonial head of state and appoints the prime minister and other ministers representing the majority party, as well as other top officials such as judges. For the most part, however, executive authority is exercised by the prime minister and other ministers, who are collectively responsible to parliament.

The parliamentary rule in Singapore is remarkable because of the fact that the PAP has been ruling the country for six decades without any significant opposition, whereas the alternative Workers' Party, Singapore Democratic Alliance and Singapore Democratic Party have never posed any threat to its position. As a result, despite the formal existence of several parties, the country has developed a ruling party system similar to that in Japan, which has largely secured the political stability required to implement a long-term economic policy.

Since Singapore had originally been a territory lacking investments or any developed small- or medium-sized businesses, its government had to be actively involved in the development of the country. During the 1960s, a number of stated-owned corporations were established, such as the Housing and Development Board, the Economic Development Board, the Community Business Board, the Central Provident Fund, Jurong Town Corporation, the Development Bank of Singapore and the Port Authority of Singapore. In 1974, the government set up Temasek Holdings Ltd. (THL) as a tool allowing it to manage hundreds of government-related companies by investing funds in them.

THL's activities cover banking, telecommunications, IT, airlines, power generation, managing the seaport and even the mass media. The THL-controlled companies account for about 10 per cent of the total production in Singapore.

The country is so influenced by the public administration that good governance conceptually pierces through the whole society. One of its key principles is meritocracy. However, it is usually perceived as a system of qualification examinations, tests and particular requirements for a civil service nomination. However, Singapore has a deeper understanding of the concept. Meritocracy begins with education, and if not all the citizens have an equal right and access to a high-quality education, meritocracy will be a useless term. The choice of public servants should be among the highest number of citizens possible, so that the best one gets the job and the most talented have an opportunity to reveal their talents for higher competiveness. Meritocracy in Singapore is based on pragmatism as an ideological and theoretical basis, founded on undiscussable devotion to market principles without any social engineering policy and classical social welfarism.

The Buddhist model

Worldwide, 520 million people identify themselves as Buddhists. Given the aforementioned mixed and dispersed nature of religious groups in the countries of Southeast and South Asia, it is often difficult to determine the civilizational affiliation of a given state. For instance, Buddhists account for the majority of the population in Korea, but statehood in the country evolved under the great influence of Confucianism. At the same time, China, while being a Confucian state, is home to the largest number of Buddhists (244 million). In Japan, most believers associate themselves with both Buddhism and Shintoism. Thus, Buddhism has influenced certain states located outside of its own civilizational domain, which includes Bhutan, Cambodia, Laos, Mongolia, Myanmar, Sri Lanka and Thailand.

The average per capita GDP (PPP) for these countries is $10,739, more than 1.5 times below the global average of $17,914. It should be noted that these countries do not provide us with an example of breakthrough countries holding top positions in global ratings, like the UAE in Islamic civilization or Singapore in the Confucian world. The most successful Buddhist country is Thailand with a per capita GDP of $19,018, followed by Mongolia ($13,735) and Sri Lanka ($13,450). At best, the figures fluctuate around the world average levels.

Despite the fact that the key Buddhist texts do not contain a clear political philosophy, the more in-depth understanding of the doctrine allows one to formulate the political value coordinates which have influenced the relevant systems of public administration. The second part of the three-part Pali Canon (Tipitaka) – the collection of sacred Buddhist texts describing the teachings of Buddha and some elements of his biography – discloses a political ideal that supplements Buddha's soteriological doctrine relying upon the central problem of pain, for which Buddhism proposes a practical solution intended for living in the here and now. Buddha is not interested in any transcendent goals – his teaching is focused on seeing the facts of life as they really are and uprooting superstitions and useless social practices by means of reason and analysis.

Buddhism offers quite detailed descriptions of an ideal type of ruler that a head of state must live up to. For instance, in Cakkavattisihanada Sutta, or the Sutta of the Lion's Roar on the Turning of the Dhamma Wheel, Buddha tells his disciples how morality, symbolized by the Dhamma Wheel treasure, reaches its heyday, falls into decay and then regenerates itself. The wheel was a symbol of power in the class of kshatriyas (warriors), who relied upon chariots. Being brought up as kshatriya, Buddha repeatedly uses this symbol in his preaching, presenting it as the Law of Goodness. The sutta, in fact, equates the qualities of the monarch with those of society, subordinating the latter to the former. Whereas Western tradition suggests that the leader, especially in a democratic environment, is a consensual representative of society, in Buddhism, all values and standards of the society depend upon the head of state. For instance, the sutta states that a time comes when successors cease to follow the rules of goodness and the first vice that possesses first them and then ordinary people is greed. The monarch ceases to help the poor, and larceny appears. Larceny is followed by cruel punishments for thieves. People, seeing the cruelty of government, develop cruelty in themselves: they take arms and go robbing and killing.

This personification of power, concentration on the person of the monarch and belief that the entire society depends upon his personal qualities, has considerably influenced the system of public administration in Buddhist countries. Bhutan, Cambodia and Thailand are constitutional monarchies; in Thailand, however, the real power found itself in the hands of a military dictatorship in 2014. Laos and Myanmar are formally republics, but the former has a one-party system that is led by the Lao People's Revolutionary Party, and the latter has been ruled since 1962 by the military who have had, according to the Constitution, a quarter of all seats in the national parliament since 2008.

The role of the head of state is also influenced by the idea that, according to Buddhist beliefs, people were originally perfect beings devoid of larceny, lies or deceit, so the state as regulator was unnecessary. But, as human behavior worsened, they became untruthful and full of violence, and anarchy overwhelmed society. The state and the monarch, in this version, came to save the society and eliminate chaos. These ideas are somewhat reminiscent of Thomas Hobbes' concept of war of all against all, in which the state acts as a leviathan, the only actor capable of maintaining order. This position of Buddhism also contributes to the evolution of a system featuring the very high role of the head of state and the personification and centralization of power.

This can be brightly exemplified by the Kingdom of Thailand, where the monarch is perceived as the leader of the country despite the fact that the monarchy became constitutional as early as 1932. During the reign of King Rama IX (Bhumibol Adulyadej, reigned 1946–2016), prime ministers and cabinets would replace one another, but the king would remain the pillar of national unity. The tradition of autocracy, centralization and large bureaucracy is characteristic of Thailand. At the same time, irrespective of whether the military is in power or the role of the monarch is strong, the bureaucracy traditionally retains the role and status of a privileged group.

A somewhat different picture can be seen in Mongolia, where a republic relatively similar to the parliamentary system has developed. After the end of the Soviet Union, Mongolia, which had traditionally been part of the Soviet sphere of influence, started to recruit its bureaucracy based on competitive examinations rather than membership in a certain party or a career in party entities. The government found itself in a situation in which local governments experienced a permanent deficit of monetary funds and their debts for the remuneration of public servants went back at least three or four months.

Phase I of the Reform Program announced by Mongolia's government was intended to establish a reliable system for finance management, public sector reporting and free distribution of data and information. To this end, the following four objectives were determined:

1   To improve overall fiscal discipline;
2   To monitor the preparation and implementation of the state budget;
3   To enhance the performance of the public sector;
4   To ensure beneficial social effects of the reform.

Phase II of the Reform Program announced by Mongolia's government was intended to improve accountability and efficiency in the public sector, as measured by budget stability and perceivable improvements in the provision of key public services. That, in its turn, involved:

1   Strengthening the institutional potential for the implementation of budgetary reform;
2   Improving financial stability through pension reform and administrative optimization;
3   Enhancing trust for public institutions.

The reforms resulted in the centralization of budgetary management and the implementation of a single treasury account for which the finance ministry of Mongolia controlled all accounts of public institutions. That meant that government was able to monitor the volume of available financial resources on a day-to-day basis, so public servants have received their salaries on time since 2003.

In general, the government policy has been driven by the following principles:

1   The use of budgeting management and reporting models with specific targets by ministries, departments and parliamentary bodies;
2   The use of budget accrual and accounting principles by ministries, departments, parliamentary bodies and government as a whole;
3   The preparation by ministries, departments and parliamentary bodies of strategic business plans, the fulfillment of which will be reported by state secretaries and executive officers on an annual basis;
4   The integration into the system of public administration of methods and techniques from the corporate sector in order to enable accurate forecasting and management of public finance.

The Hindu model

Hinduism is the third largest religion in the world with 1.15 billion followers and is most widespread in India, Nepal and Mauritius. The average
per capita GDP (PPP) for these countries is $11,511, which is significantly
lower than the global average of $17,914. Moreover, the most successful of
these three countries is Mauritius, where this indicator is about $23,709, or
three times as high as the relevant figure for India ($7,762) and almost ten
times higher as compared to Nepal ($3,064). At the same time, India, with its
1,355,051,000 residents, ranks second in the world in terms of population.

Given the democratic nature of the country, this demographic pattern
creates a unique situation, where more than 900 million people are entitled to vote. Taking into account the specific political mobilization of its
population, producing a voter turnout of 65–70 per cent, India is the country
with the greatest number of voting citizens in the world. Demography, in
general, plays a vital role in determining a country's future, especially in
the case of India. Its population's share of working-age citizens is over 50
per cent, which will rise to 60 per cent in 2050. Some analysts insist that a
fast-growing working population will lead to a larger labor force, more sav-
ing and hence more investment. However, this view gives the demography
not only a vital role but also a status of destiny, leading to an opinion that
public policy plays little or no role. Nevertheless, if young people are not
educated and new jobs are not created, population growth by itself is not
going to add anything to the prosperity and wellbeing of the nation. India
has a critical need to generate employment and provide its citizens with
high-quality education and skills, otherwise its demography may lead to
a very complicated situation with its economy and governance in general.
Some of the reforms done as a means for a faster economic growth in reality
led to even more difficult unemployment rates. As an example, development of the industrial sector is often tied to modernization of agriculture
and its improved productivity, which leads to an increasing application of
modern technology, resulting in freeing even more labor in rural areas. So,
if an adequate demand for those workers is not motivated by the government, modernization will in reality lead to a worsening of social policy and
wellbeing of citizens.

Since gaining independence in 1947, India originally evolved as a democracy against the background of an extremely high poverty rate, ethnic and
religious tensions and, as already noted, a huge population. One of the factors which allowed India to set up a political system based on the principles
of Western democracy was the historical pattern of state-religion relations.
The Indian society of the Rig-Veda period (1700–1100 B.C.) developed a
system of social classes in which the top class, or varna, was represented

by brahmins (priests). Then followed kshatriyas (warriors), vaishyas (land-owners) and shudras (servants).

In India, therefore, in a manner similar to Western Europe, the separation of secular and religious authority occurred. The brahmins were not only a separate varna, they also enjoyed a higher status than the warriors. Of course, the degree of their organization and institutionalization was lower than that of the Catholic Church, but their moral authority was beyond the jurisdiction of the state, because the brahmins were deemed the guardians of the sacred law that had existed before, and independently from, the exist-ing political authority. In contrast to a number of other civilizations, Indian monarchs were considered not the creators and interpreters of sacred texts but only their subjects, who had to respect the rules of behavior established in such texts and monitored by priests. That provided the basis for the evo-lution of a society whose characteristics were similar to Western ones. Of course, we refer only to the political values and organization of state power, since Indian society itself is fundamentally different from Western society in terms of both its values and its structure; it is sufficient to mention the continued existence of the untouchables, that has no analog in Abrahamic religions.

India is a union including 28 states and nine union territories (the latter, in contrast to states, have no regional government and are governed directly by the federal authorities). The union government consists of the executive, the legislative and the judicial branches, which are represented, respectively, by the prime minister, parliament and the supreme court. This structure is replicated in the regional governments, which also consist of the executive, the legislative and the judicial branches. The legal system applicable at the federal and regional levels is based on English case and statutory law.

After it gained independence in 1947, India encountered tremendous social and economic problems. Despite the absence of a power vacuum due to the efficient administrative system built by the British and taken over by local governments, the country needed a series of reforms in order to meet challenges relating to public administration. In the 1990s, after a policy of economic liberalization and restructuring had been adopted in India, a number of expert committees were set up (the Raja Chelliah committee on tax reform, the Rangarajan committee on foreign investments, the Gos-wami committee on industry and corporative restructuring) to examine and prepare recommendations for various policy measures relating to economic reform. Despite the large-scale activities of the said committees and the deregulation of certain economy sectors, due to the high involvement of public authorities in the documentation and implementation of investments, this area continues to be a problem for the government of India. At the same time, the voices of new-generation politicians, who treat the bureaucracy as an obstacle to the achievement of their political goals, are growing ever louder. On the one hand, this results in frequent conflicts between the political leaders and the permanent staff of the executive authorities. But the same process has also led to the politicization of the bureaucracy, which has found itself involved in conflicts with various political forces and groups instead of pursuing the goals set by its elected superiors.

In this regard, one of the key tasks in the context of reforming was to reduce the share of the state in the economy by lifting excessive controls, reducing investments in the public sector and privatizing and outsourcing many services that had traditionally been provided by the state. The role of government in such a system should be limited to defining a framework policy of public administration rather than administration itself. One of the goals of the reform was to ensure equal rules of play between the public and the private economy sectors, as well as between domestic and foreign companies. That was rather difficult to achieve in a situation where prices for many classes of goods and services were determined by administrative rather than market-based mechanisms. In today's India, however, the public sector tends to act as an intermediary in economic activities that provide infrastructure, invest in the social sector and address poverty issues.

Recruitment in India is run in several stages, including involvement of qualified candidates through vacancies being published as advertisements, selection of candidates by a competitive examination and placement of selected individuals after issuance of appointment letters to them conveyed through a competent authority. To accomplish those steps, an independent recruiting agency was created. In the states, those functions are performed by the Public Service Commissions.

Official recruitment is done internally through promotion from within and externally through a competitive examination.

The Japanese model

Japan is one of the most developed countries in the world; it successfully implements new technologies, creates innovations and boasts high living standards. In terms of per capita GDP (PPP), it is among the top 30 countries ($42,794 against the global average of about $17,000). Its average life expectancy of 84.2 years ranks first in the world.

As already mentioned, Japan is a unique country, and we can hardly include it in one of the currently existing civilizations. In this state, people identify themselves as both Buddhists and Shintoists – followers of their traditional religion based on the animistic beliefs of the ancient Japanese, involving the worshipping of numerous deities and spirits of the dead. In addition, one cannot ignore the strong influence of the Confucian tradition that has largely shaped the political culture of the nation.

Japan is a constitutional monarchy, in which the emperor's power is very limited. He plays a ceremonial role, being, according to the Constitution, the symbol of the nation and of people's unity. Executive power in the country belongs mainly to the prime minister and his cabinet. Since the country uses a parliamentary model of cabinet formation, political parties and parliament itself play a key role. Similar to Confucian Singapore, the Liberal Democratic Party has been ruling Japan almost uninterruptedly since 1955. The only exceptions were periods between 1993 and 1994 and between 2009 and 2012.

The system of public administration in Japan is believed to be one of the most efficient bureaucracies in the world. In Japan, in contrast to many other models, including Western ones, the most talented and skilled staff is concentrated in the public sector.

However, this breakthrough pattern of Japan's development involves a number of problems as well. The academic and professional community discusses whether it is possible to harmonize an efficient public administration and democracy. Traditionally, any optimization of public service was perceived in the country as the need to reasonably reduce the number of employees and their administrative units. Since the end of the 20th century, however, Japan has been emphasizing not only cutting costs and relaxing administrative pressure, but also involving citizens in the process of discussing and making public decisions.

The economic and financial success Japan had enjoyed until the 1990s was mainly due to the efforts of its government. But, as a financial crisis in Asia began, the Japanese economy was shaken, largely as a result of the national administration's decisions regarding investments in the domestic economy and neighboring countries. Japan was forced to move toward decentralization and depart from a model in which the government was to secure economic growth.

The government consolidated 80 institutions into the Independent Administrative Corporation. This included monetary agencies, print shops, hospitals, national museums and laboratories. The principal goal of this measure was to separate the policy-making function from policy implementation and to implement innovations as part of the service provision for citizens by enhancing the autonomy and accountability of the institutions and ensuring the transparency of their operations. The corporation is funded out of the national budget, and some of its employees have the status of public servants.

In the early 2000s, a special board for discussing the system of public service issued its report on ways to reform the state bureaucracy. It proposed a concept based on meritocratic principles for bureaucracy recruitment and operation, such as a special system of entry examinations and performance-driven remuneration. Exchanging experience between the public and the private sectors was encouraged as well.

Nevertheless, despite all efforts within the country, one of its essential problems continues to be central. Bureaucracy and politics, as in a number of other Asian systems, are not only unseparated but also merged to such an extent that ever more people wonder whether the mammoth staff of public servants can, in principle, be controlled by the legislature or the executive. In order to reduce the role of its bureaucracy, the country continuously carries out decentralization reforms, but it appears that the Japanese political culture itself does not put any stress on mechanisms for the separation of power or for the implementation of checks and counterbalances that are characteristic of the Western model and is more concerned with the need to maximize efficiency – a task the system copes with in an almost perfect manner.

Japan implements the e-Japan strategy, aimed principally at improving the quality of public services. Its ministries and departments provide public access not only to their own decisions, but also to comments by their advisory boards, including negative ones.

The portals of public authorities include forums, at which citizens may register themselves, take part in discussing any proposed decisions and make their own proposals. In 2006, one of the targets set by the Japanese government was that online processing should cover 50 per cent of the total number of applications to state and municipal authorities. It became clear by 2010 that the very formulation of the problem was incorrect, since online applications were printed out and then processed. It was necessary to reform the whole business process in the field of public services.

After the Liberal Democratic Party regained power in 2013, Shinzo Abe's cabinet has achieved a major breakthrough in the digitalization of public services. The national government has developed the unified governmental platform Kasumigaseki Cloud in order to support a unified data and information base and to cut costs. A local government network (LGWAN) has also enabled information exchange among the municipal bodies, as well as between them and the national authorities. Cloud computing and other IT services constitute the basis for the Japanese e-government.

The introduction of the My Number system as a key tool for any administrative procedure relating to social security and taxation has significantly facilitated communications between citizens and the relevant authorities. A similar system involving the pension insurance number and the individual taxpayer number is used in Russia. By using My Number, citizens can not only see any incoming communications from the government but also send applications to it to obtain documents, excerpts or various public services via an online portal. When evaluating the results of these reforms, many experts observe that, despite the breakthrough nature of the implemented form and mechanisms for service provision, digitalization still remains an easier mode of interaction with public authorities for more affluent socio-economic groups, whereas the poorer segments of population are beyond the coverage of the e-government.

Questions for self-study:

1   Please compare the role of political parties in the public administration systems of India, China and Japan.
2   Please examine the experience of administrative reform in China. How does it correlate with the global trends in public administration?
3   Please consider the distribution of the population in South and South-east Asia in terms of its religious and cultural affiliations.

Additional materials:

Hori, M. *Japanese Public Administration and Its Adaptation to New Public Management*. ResearchGate. 2018
Sarkar, S. *Public Administration in India*. PHI Learning Pvt. Ltd. 2018
Lee, K.F. *AI Superpowers: China, Silicon Valley and the New World Order*. Houghton Mifflin Harcourt; 1 edition. 2018

2.5 The African model of public administration

The term "Africa" is too broad for describing the civilization Huntington wrote about. Geographically, the African continent accommodates states whose ethnic basis is made up of Arabs belonging to Islamic civilization; Ethiopians, who represent one of the most ancient Christian churches; the followers of local religious cults of a shamanistic or animistic nature and so on. Referring to "African" countries, we typically mean the states south of the Sahara populated by the Negroid race, although a given nation may be equally split between Christianity and Islam. But the key fact is that neither the former nor the latter religion is a determining factor in the cultural genesis of the African peoples.

As a preliminary remark, it should be noted that the borders of the sub-Saharan states are arbitrary and, in contrast to the traditional model of nation state, do not define a territory inhabited by a homogenous population speaking the same language, sharing a common system of values and so on.

The region is home to more than 3,000 different ethnic groups speaking over 2,100 different tongues and living in 46 states south of the Sahara.

The world religions, primarily Christianity and Islam, are widespread in Africa, but, as compared to other regions in which they are practiced, they are considerably modified by local religious cults, traditions and beliefs. Sects and local religious groups unrelated to the official denominations of the Abrahamic religions are common as well.

The average per capita GDP (PPP) in these states is equal to $4,929, or almost four times lower than the global average. More importantly, the bottom ten countries in terms of this indicator, according to the World Bank's statistics, are in Africa: Gambia ($1,706), Madagascar ($1,634), Sierra Leone ($1,604), Mozambique ($1,328), Malawi ($1,309), Liberia ($1,306), Niger ($1,048), Democratic Republic of Congo ($931), Central African Republic ($872) and Burundi ($738).

The population of the African countries south of the Sahara has grown from 186 million to 856 million between 1950 and 2010, about 11 million each year during the last 60 years or about 670 million over the 60-year period. By 2060, the African population south of the Sahara could reach 2.7 billion. To compare, Europe anticipates a population decrease from 738 million in 2010 to 702 million in 2060.

Nigeria, Ethiopia, Tanzania, Democratic Republic of Congo, Niger, Zambia and Uganda, along with China and India, will be the most populous countries in the world. As predicted, Nigeria's population will exceed that of the US by approximately 30 million by 2050.

The death rate, especially among children, is falling. Infant mortality figures have decreased from 183/1,000 for the children born between 1950 and 1955 to 69/1,000 for the children born between 2010 and 2015. Life expectancy has increased from 36 years in the period of 1950–1955 to 56 years nowadays.

The countries which have succeeded in pushing down both their mortality and their fertility levels increasingly discover that young people account for the majority of their population. The average age of people in Niger, Uganda and Chad is below 16. Of the ten countries of the world with the youngest populations, eight are situated in the sub-Saharan part of Africa, and all ten states will be confined to this region by 2050.

Demographic data of this kind is not encouraging. What will be the life of the people who will be born in Africa during this period? Will they live in their own countries, or will humankind see a mass migration of African residents northward? This is largely dependent upon public administration in these countries. Despite that, in recent years, some countries of the continent have initiated reforms involving leading international experts and arranged for international forums and congresses in order to find solutions for African countries; but the situation largely remains extremely grave.

Most countries in the region emerged during the period of decolonization in Africa between 1950 and 1970. Originally, the constitutions of these countries were based on the fundamental laws of their former metropolitan nations. But soon it became obvious that the socio-cultural conditions in, say, Cameroon and France significantly differed from each other and the constitutional laws did not meet the necessary consensus in the society. Some countries began to use socialist models for their constitutions.

The socialist model of constitutions refers to the type of fundamental law that was applied in the Soviet Union and the countries of the socialist bloc. Its key features are the unity of the legislative and the executive branches of government, in contrast to their separation in the liberal model; political monism, in contrast to political pluralism; and the sovereignty of the working class, in contrast to popular sovereignty.

Other countries used liberal models adapted to local realities. But the problems facing the countries in Africa south of the Sahara were somewhat different from those of most countries in the world during that period. The initial building of public institutions was on the agenda.

Colonialism has been the key and decisive factor in the development of modern public administration in African countries. The Europeans drew borders between the countries and provided tools and systems for governance and the bureaucracy and education for local leaders. The Europeans traditionally used power in order to set up, review and determine rules and institutions, and that had nothing to do with the local mechanisms for control.

The overwhelming majority of the population still adheres to the primarily traditional rituals and norms of behavior. Under these circumstances, post-colonial states, seeking to emulate the Western traditions of governance, continue their attempts to launch public institutions characteristic of a Western society; since these attempts do not rely upon any social or cultural basis in the society, this results in economic and social fragmentation and contributes to the crisis of state-building, administration and economic development in Africa.

Before British colonization in the 19th century, the region knew some authority, but the powers of its traditional leaders were rather informal and had never been codified or reflected in legislation.

> **Codification** means the systematization of legal norms in the course
> of law-creating activities and the publication of a consolidated, legally
> and logically consistent act on this basis.

Each community was independent from another, being ruled by chiefs
who provided security and protection against external aggression. But
the post-colonial states were based on the elements and institutions of
colonialism, such as the weak vertical and horizontal integration of the
countries, the domination of governments based on force rather than
authority and the low responsibility of government to the population.
The budgetary and administrative systems in Zimbabwe and Tanzania
have undergone practically no changes since the independence of these
states.

The World Bank traditionally pays attention to the drastic poverty in the
African countries that they are often unable to address. The absence of any
real production growth results in a steady decline in living standards and
per capita income. The inefficiency of public institutions is usually cited as
the root cause of these troubles. Private sector initiative and market-based
mechanisms prove useless, if neither a stable system of public service nor a
reliable judicial system exists.

Another important problem is that public institutions suffer from a lack
of funding. It is typically explained by the absence of a financial basis
in these countries. But often the elites themselves are uninterested in the
development of stable and evolving institutions. In the field of education,
for instance, they are reluctant to promote the establishment of efficient
educational institutions, whose activities could trigger changes in society
and then in the policies of the country. Obsolete political institutions in
developing countries fear an efficient bureaucracy, because it threatens
to evolve into alternative power centers in the society. Furthermore, one
should not ignore the fact that, as estimated by the African Union, 25 per
cent of the African states' aggregate GDP, or $148 billion, is lost to cor-
ruption each year.

After they gained independence, many African countries have passed
through a series of economic and financial crises, especially since the
beginning of the 1970s. For most of them, poverty and economic stagnation
remain pressing issues and the balance of payment is of extreme concern,
along with the heavy debt burden and the level of public expenditures in
relation to the dwindling sources of revenues and the growing cost of public
services.

> **Stagnation** (from Latin *stagnatio*, "immobility") means a situation in the economy where production and trade do not grow over a long period of time, the unemployment rate rises and wages and living standards decrease.

These factors triggered attempts to carry out reforms according to the principles of New Public Management in order to reduce the role of government. However, whereas such measures resulted in enhancing the role of the private sector in Western states, it is easy to guess, given the fundamentally different condition of this sector in the African countries, what the result of such reforms was there.

Reforms in Africa, which started in the 1980s, mainly began with the structural adjustment programs (SAPs). Before that the main focus had been a so-called Africanization of the small colonial civil services left after the metropolises done in parallel with its expansion through aid by the former colonial powers by training and technical assistance. The loans of the 1980s were used mainly for stabilizing crises of balance of payments and fiscal deficits, inflation and currency overvaluations.

The main results of the 1980s civil service reform were the downsizing of the workforce through mergers, recruitment freezes and the elimination of ghost workers, which led to attempts to use savings on recruitment to pay higher salaries to higher-level managers with better skills.

In the 1990s, a different approach was taken as it became evident that downsizing and pay restructuring were not producing the desired results without other necessary steps. The reduction of civil service went along with a need to restructure the civil services, focusing on management systems, performance and budget/financial management and the marketization of service delivery. This is the particular period when an attempt was made to transfer to African countries all the techniques of public sector reform which are known as New Public Management. In particular, high-level reform agencies were created, guided by the presidential or prime ministerial offices, and were backed up by teams of foreign consultants and technical assistance personnel.

The reforms after the 1990s mainly focused on creating a responsive and legitimate state for sustaining an effective market economy, by also improving service delivery to citizens. Poverty reduction strategy plans were launched as a new condition for loans to heavily indebted poor countries (HIPCs), the majority of which are located in Africa. Public servants had to develop programs with engagement of opinions and demands of the public and designing their own performance improvement plans (PIPs), creating service delivery standards monitored by both responsible managers and citizen user groups.

The same logic was behind attempts to modify the political systems existing in many countries of the continent. An unstable political order nudged people toward the idea that it was necessary to transform public administration to create basic systems of governance, have more democratic institutions, develop a civic society and implement the rule of law principle, a transparent and accountable government and a reliable and independent judiciary. Obviously, none of the previously listed institutions and mechanisms emerged in the Western countries merely because they were stipulated in a constitution. All of them have resulted from the evolution of social institutions based on the Western Christian culture, which does not constitute the ideological and theoretical foundation of African societies.

Moreover, the replication of the standardized bureaucratic procedures, which have been established in European countries over several centuries, often leads to government incapability in countries south of the Sahara. The complex institutional mechanisms, which, in the West, ensure the operation of checks and counterbalances and prevent the usurpation of power by one person or entity with the support of powerful civic society institutions, political parties and regional and municipal authorities, impede the timely and efficient implementation of various strategies in African states.

> **Usurpation** (from Latin *usurpatio*, "appropriation") means the forced, unlawful takeover of power or appropriation of other people's rights or authorities.

Many local governments have complained that they are unable to respond to global and national challenges in an efficient manner. It should also be understood that the nature of problems that governments are forced to solve in Africa somewhat differs from the typically cosmetic reforms in European countries, where the management decisions required from governments are several times less numerous and less pressing than in developing countries.

Decentralization by the local governments can be deemed another Western approach in reforming public administration in African countries. Various methods have been used to implement it. One method is to delegate some administrative functions to a lower tier of government. Despite that in general this measure is not frequent, it is quite common in certain areas, such as agriculture, primary education and preventive health care. For example, the central government in Botswana has set up and supervises district councils as well as a national council for the development of rural areas in order to coordinate and implement measures to develop rural areas and address droughts.

One example of such policy is Ghana, where a decentralization process has led to the establishment of district assemblies concerned with how best to manage their business successfully within the administrative and political system in which they function. It is therefore important that an efficient leadership and management team exists at the local level that employs the limited resources at its disposal to meet the prioritized development needs of people in the local areas. Metropolitan, municipal and district assemblies (MMDAs) in Ghana largely rely on national fiscal transfers from the central government for the development of their territorial jurisdictions.

One of the key reforms of Ghana in that sense is that all stakeholders must be made aware of the total national revenue out of which the 5 per cent is set aside as a District Assembly Common Fund (DACF) and the quantum of the 5 per cent must also be made known to all stakeholders, as one of the major problems is the incapability to plan the budgeting due to an ad hoc distribution of finance. Experts recommend that steps be taken to put the DACF formula in line with the budget preparation process of MMDAs. It is noted that the DACF formula sanction must be part of the budget preparation process, not part of its execution process. The budget should be submitted to parliament during the first quarter of the fiscal year for approval.

Many experts in general consider, however, that decentralization reforms result in the proliferation of local-level institutions, but fail to bring the state closer to the people, as the majority of African states don't have strong control over distant territories and usually rely on informal and traditional authorities to access local populations.

Another method of decentralization is "agencification", according to which a solid bureaucracy is divided into agencies. In particular, South Africa and Zambia have established independent tax authorities with corporate procedures of management in order to increase the efficiency and accountability of tax collection operations.

Sometimes certain decision-making powers are delegated to entities that are outside the normal bureaucratic framework and only indirectly controlled by the government, such as regional development corporations and semi-autonomous agencies. According to this approach, a more business-like structure is used to perform governmental functions, with the implementation of audit and accounting arrangements from the business area.

Audit means activities involving the examination of financial accounts and accounting data and, following such examination, the preparation of a reasoned independent opinion regarding the accuracy of such accounts in the form of a written auditors' statement.

In Kenya, for instance, public corporations were used to initiate, finance and manage large-scale agricultural projects, such as tea production. Lesotho has established a semi-public body to finance and manage a large project of water resource development in the mountainous districts of the country. Botswana and Ghana have set up autonomous hospitals with independent governing boards to enhance the efficiency of services.

According to a common practice, decision-making powers are delegated to lower-level bodies or officials, thus encouraging them to assume full responsibility without approaching the delegating authority. This includes financial capabilities, as well as powers to put together and implement development projects and programs.

The largest-scale form of decentralization is devolution, which allows the lower tiers of administration to make decisions without the involvement of the central government. For instance, Ghana implements a public finance management program entrusting managers with higher control over budgets. In Ethiopia, broad legislative, executive, judicial and fiscal powers are fully devolved to the regional authorities.

In all the aforementioned cases, decentralization is meant to provide a mechanism allowing the population to participate in the process of administration, as well as the basis for representing community interests in governmental decision-making entities.

Another common form of decentralization is privatization, which is understood as the transfer of operational control and responsibility from the public sector to the private one, that is, to non-governmental organizations or private businesses.

In a broader sense, privatization covers a wide range of governmental measures and policies encouraging the involvement of the private sector in the provision of public services and eliminating or modifying the monopolistic status of public enterprises. Privatization may be a complex process, often inconsistent with the need to increase financial and economic efficiency and disapproved of by political opposition.

Despite the fact that various African countries have been taking all of these measures during a rather long period, one cannot say that the local authorities have achieved any remarkable success. Apart from certain achievements in addressing particular problems and certain successful projects, these decades cannot be seen as a watershed period for Africa, given the systemic crisis of governance models and statehood on the continent.

Since the local governments are unable to overcome their acute social and economic problems as well as to set up the operations of relatively stable institutions, the international community and individual developed countries take steps to assist the African states. This can be exemplified by the Good Financial Governance program supported by Germany's Agency for International Cooperation to increase the efficiency of public finance spending and management in Africa. It does this by providing more accurate assessments as to where budgetary flows are directed and using external audits to identify common problems. In addition to the technical aspects of public finance governance, the program also includes regulatory, political and economic aspects. The analysis includes the processes of budget spending both by the central government staff and by industry-specific ministries, their departments and other agencies, determining finance governance risk areas. This model has been tested in several African countries, including Ghana, Kenya, Malawi, Mozambique, Senegal, Tanzania and Uganda.

Decision-making models based on risk assessment are increasingly used in managing environmental protection, including the exploitation of natural resources:

- The allocation of water intake licenses;
- Urban planning and building control;
- Flood risk management;
- Air and water pollution monitoring;
- Waste management;
- The extraction of mineral resources and so on.

Fighting natural disasters and addressing emergency situations or climate change involve an integrated risk assessment both within and outside the relevant ecosystems.

The African Risk Capacity, an African Union specialized agency, was established to help African governments better plan, prepare and respond to extreme weather conditions and natural disasters. Through collaboration and innovative finance, the ARC enables countries to strengthen their disaster risk management systems and access rapid financing when disaster strikes to protect their food security and the livelihoods of their population.

The ARC mission is to use up-to-date financing mechanisms, such as risk pooling and risk transfer, to create pan-African systems for responding to climate change that enable African countries to meet the needs of those affected by natural disasters.

As a rule, international efforts toward the improvement of the public administration system in African countries are focused on a number of aspects.

- Political management: news coverage of elections, support for representative bodies, the mass media and civic society;
- Administrative management: central government and interdepartmental coordination, public service reform, decentralization and intragovernmental communication;
- Economic management: collection of statistics, strategic planning, assistance coordination and improving legal regulation for the development of the private sector;
- Justice and security: strengthening security institutions and upgrading the judicial system;
- Local governance: creating decentralized local entities and strengthening provincial and local administrations.

In the context of African public administration, problems of governance run much deeper than can be addressed by the Western attitude toward providing public sector accountability. Many states lack popular backing and legitimacy, and this has fundamental consequences for how they operate. Many experts mention that political power in Africa is not derived from the formal institutions of the state, nor is it legitimized by the provision of public services. It is rather the patron–client networks organized through ethnic communities that operate as the main sources of political power.

It would be a misunderstanding, however, to think that it is caused by weak civil society or insufficient civic mobilization. Apparently, civic participation is unlikely to have strong political consequences. The majority of African public administration systems do not offer efficient models of inclusion for different interest groups in decision-making. Even in countries considered to be multiparty democracies such as Benin, Ghana and Senegal, political parties mainly rely on clientelist mobilization strategies. Political clientelism is even more obvious in ethnically polarized countries, such as Kenya. While power sharing based on ethnic factors is widespread in Africa, it leads to elite-level bargains. Clientelism and ethnic polarization makes state institutions serve and provide services for different groups in society unequally. It is not for a lack of prospects for political participation that citizens are alienated from the state, but due rather to the low possibility of difference to be made through their participation in a political system.

Questions for self-study:

1   What countries belong to Africa south of the Sahara? Why are these countries allocated to a separate group?
2   Please analyze the distribution of the continent's states in terms of their belonging to colonial empires. How did the metropolitan states influence public administration in their colonies?
3   Please consider the positions of the African states in the Human Development Index and the Fragile States Index.

Additional materials:

Abramova, I.O. *Africa's Population in the New Global Economy*. Moscow: RAS Institute for African Studies. 2010
Lukamba-Muhiya, S.V.D. and E. Peprah Ababio Tshombe. *Public Administration in Africa: Performance and Challenges*. Routledge. 2017
Nhema, A. Public Administration and the Development of Africa: A Critical Assessment. *Journal of Public Administration and Governance*. 2016

Notes

1   J. Schumpeter. *Capitalism, Socialism, and Democracy: Third Edition* (Harper Perennial Modern Thought). Harper Perennial Modern Classics. 2008
2   G. Sartori. *The Theory of Democracy Revisited: Part One: The Contemporary Debate*, Vol. 1. CQ Press; 1 edition. 1987
3   L. Canfora. *Democracy in Europe: A History of an Ideology*. John Wiley & Sons. 2008
4   V.M. Gribovsky. *People and Power in the Byzantine State. An Experience of Historical Dogmatic Research*. St. Petersburg. 1897. p. 342
5   http://docs.cntd.ru/search/ykazprezidenta/year/2018
6   www.federalregister.gov/presidential-documents/executive-orders
7   Muhtasar Sahih Muslim. In 2 vols. Imam Al-Munziri. – Almaty: Kausar Sayahat LLP. 2013. Mode of access: https://archive.org/stream/muslim.kausar-sayahat/muslim.kausar-sayahat.1_djvu.txt
8   Ibid., Had. 1852
9   B. Bammarny. The Caliphate State in Theory and Practice. *Arab Law Quarterly*. 2017. Vol. 31 (2). pp. 163–186
10 D. Chirot. The War Against Modernity: The Theology and Politics of Contemporary Muslim Extremism. *Mir Rossii*. 2017. Vol. 26 (1). pp. 127–151

Conclusion

The beginning of the 21st century has seen the decline of the illusion that any universal models can exist. Economists, political scientists, legal scholars, sociologists and researchers in dozens of other fields of science have begun to investigate the reasons for which the institutional models that are so successful and that lead to the formation of a mass consumption society do not work in certain countries.

Public administration, although a field of educational and research activities relatively new to our country, is also affected by this process. The idea that the training of public servants throughout the world should be limited to adapting the practices and mechanisms well established in Western countries has proved to be incorrect. The transition from the classic model of public administration to New Public Management and then to Public Governance has not been embraced globally and remains the trajectory of development characteristic of not even the entire Western world but a small part of it, the Anglo-Saxon states.

That being said, many elements of up-to-date public administration technologies have been replicated in various civilizations to the extent that they could find an appropriate social base for their implementation in the local cultures. The only question is which well-known structures of public administration could be built on a given socio-cultural foundation and which could not, so that local alternatives should be developed instead.

It is obvious that, despite globalization and the immense volume of data accessible to humankind, the differences among nations are still here. Moreover, the universal accessibility of any information source conspicuously demonstrates the great extent to which various civilizations are different from each other. This, in turn, only means that no simple ways exist to solve the problems facing public administration and that unique methods taking into account the experience of any particular state are required.

Bibliography

Abramova, I.O. *Africa's Population in the New Global Economy*. Moscow: RAS Institute for African Studies. 2010

Alekseyeva, T.A. Strategic Culture: Evolution of the Concept – Polis. *Political Studies*. 2012. Vol. 5. pp. 130–147

Almond, A. and S. Verba. *The Civic Culture: Political Attitudes and Democracy in Five Nations*. SAGE Publications. 1989

Bammarny, B. The Caliphate State in Theory and Practice. *Arab Law Quarterly*. 2017. Vol. 31 (2). pp. 163–186

Canfora, L. *Democracy in Europe: A History of an Ideology*. John Wiley & Sons. 2008

Chandler, J. and M. Dent. *Questioning the New Public Management*. Taylor & Francis Limited. 2019

Chirot, D. The War Against Modernity: The Theology and Politics of Contemporary Muslim Extremism. *Mir Rossii*. 2017. Vol. 26 (1). pp. 127–151

Durkheim, E. *Moral Education: A Study in the Theory and Application of the Sociology of Education*. Literary Licensing, LLC. 2011

European Commission. *Quality of Public Administration. A Toolbox for Practitioners*. Directorate-General for Employment, Social Affairs and Inclusion Unit E.1. 2015

Geertz, C. *The Interpretation of Cultures*. Basic Books; 3 edition. 2017

Gribovsky, V.M. *People and Power in the Byzantine State. An Experience of Historical Dogmatic Research*. St. Petersburg. 1897. p. 342

Guiso, L., P. Sapienza and L. Zingales. Does Culture Affect Economic Outcomes? *Journal of Economic Perspectives, American Economic Association*. 2006. Vol. 20 (2). pp. 23–48. Spring

Harris, J. *The Lost World of Byzantium*. New Haven and London: Yale University Press. 2015

Hori, M. *Japanese Public Administration and Its Adaptation to New Public Management*. ResearchGate. 2018

Huntington, S.P. *The Third Wave: Democratization in the Late 20th Century (Volume 4) the Julian J. Rothbaum Distinguished Lecture Series*. University of Oklahoma Press. 1993

Huntington, S.P. *The Clash of Civilizations and the Remaking of World Order*. Simon & Schuster. 2011

Jaspers, K. *The Origin and Goal of History (Routledge Revivals)*. Routledge. 2014

Juneja, P. *Structural Functional Approach to Public Administration*. Management Study Guide. 2019.

Kuz'bozhev, E.N. and I.A. Koz'eva. *The History of Public Administration in Russia*. Moscow: YURAIT. 2015

Lee, K.F. *AI Superpowers: China, Silicon Valley and the New World Order*. Houghton Mifflin Harcourt; 1 edition. 2018

Lukamba-Muhiya, S.V.D. and E. Peprah Ababio Tshombe. *Public Administration in Africa: Performance and Challenges*. Routledge. 2017

Massey, A. and K. Johnston. *The International Handbook of Public Administration and Governance*. Edward Elgar Publishing. 2015

Muhtasar Sahih Muslim. In 2 vols. Imam Al-Munziri. – Almaty: Kausar Sayahat LLP. 2013. Mode of access: https://archive.org/stream/muslim.kausar-sayahat/muslim.kausar-sayahat.1_djvu.txt

Nhema, A. Public Administration and the Development of Africa: A Critical Assessment. *Journal of Public Administration and Governance*. 2016

Nietzsche, F. *The Will to Power*. Courier Dover Publications. 2019

Nisnevich, Y.A., A.V. Malashenko and A.V. Ryabov. *The Rise of a Post-Industrial Civilization: From Digitalisation to Barbarism*. Moscow: YURAIT. 2019

Pettit, P. *Republicanism: A Theory of Freedom and Government*. Oxford: Oxford University Press. 1999

Pollitt, C. and G. Bouckaert. *Public Management Reform. A Comparative Analysis – Into the Age of Austerity*. Oxford: Oxford University Press. 2017

Samier, E. The Islamic Public Administration Tradition: Historical, Theoretical and Practical Dimensions. *Halduskultuur*. 2017

Sarkar, S. *Public Administration in India*. PHI Learning Pvt. Ltd. 2018

Sartori, G. *The Theory of Democracy Revisited: Part One: The Contemporary Debate*, Vol. 1. CQ Press; 1 edition. 1987

Schumpeter, J. *Capitalism, Socialism, and Democracy: Third Edition* (Harper Perennial Modern Thought). Harper Perennial Modern Classics. 2008

Sorokin, P.A. *On the Practice of Sociology* (Heritage of Sociology Series). Chicago: University of Chicago Press; 1 edition. 1998

Torfing, J., L.B. Andersen, K.K. Klausen and C. Greve. *Public Governance Paradigms: Competing and Co-Existing*. Edward Elgar Publishing, Incorporated. 2020

Torkunov, A.V. *Along the Road to the Future – 2.5*. Moscow: LKI. 2017

Toynbee, A.J. *A Study of History*. Oxford: Oxford University Press; 1 edition. 1947

Toynbee, A.J. *Civilisation at Trial. The World and the West*. World Publishing Company. 1968

UNDP. *From Old Public Administration to the New Public Service*. UNDP. 2015

von Hayek, A., D. Antiseri and L. Infantino. *Conoscenza, competizione e libertà* (Italiano). Rubbettino; 1 edition. 1998

Weber, M. The Three Types of Legitimate Rule. *Berkeley Publications in Society and Institutions*. 1958. Vol. 4 (1)

Yenghibaryan, R.V. *21th Century: An Islamic Challenge*. Moscow: Norma. 2016

Auxiliary materials

Countries by per capita GDP (PPP) (World Bank data)

#	Country	2018
1	Qatar	126,598
2	Luxembourg	111,103
3	Singapore	101,353
4	Ireland	83,203
5	Brunei	80,778
6	UAE	74,943
7	Kuwait	73,705
8	Switzerland	68,096
9	San Marino	
10	Norway	65,599
11	United States of America	62,641
12	Iceland	57,311
13	Netherlands	56,329
14	Austria	55,510
15	Saudi Arabia	55,120
16	Denmark	55,105
17	Germany	53,735
18	Sweden	52,725
19	Australia	51,602
20	Belgium	50,367
21	Canada	48,107
22	Finland	47,930
23	Bahrain	47,220
24	United Kingdom	45,489
25	France	45,342
26	Japan	42,794
27	Malta	42,567
28	Italy	41,630
29	Oman	41,435
30	New Zealand	41,026
31	Republic of Korea	40,112

#	Country	2018
32	Spain	39,915
33	Israel	39,822
34	Czech Republic	39,744
35	Aruba	
36	Cyprus	
37	Slovenia	38,209
38	Estonia	35,450
39	Lithuania	35,343
40	Slovakia	33,917
41	Portugal	33,041
42	Bahamas	
43	Trinidad and Tobago	32,228
44	Saint Kitts and Nevis	31,831
45	Malaysia	31,698
46	Poland	31,343
47	Latvia	30,692
48	Hungary	30,673
49	Seychelles	30,503
50	Greece	29,592
51	Curacao	
52	Romania	28,206
53	Turkey	27,893
54	Kazakhstan	27,831
55	Croatia	27,505
56	Russia	27,147
57	Antigua and Barbuda	26,739
58	Cuba	
59	Panama	25,509
60	Turks and Caicos	25,326
61	Chile	25,223
62	Mauritius	23,709
63	Uruguay	23,531
64	Equatorial Guinea	23,473
65	Iran	
66	Bulgaria	21,960
67	Libya	20,706
68	Argentina	20,567
69	Montenegro	20,495
70	Belarus	19,960
71	Mexico	19,888
72	Barbados	
73	Palau	19,353
74	Turkmenistan	19,270
75	Thailand	19,018
76	Botswana	18,583
77	China	18,210
78	Azerbaijan	18,012

(*Continued*)

(Continued)

#	Country	2018
79	Gabon	17,912
80	Venezuela	
81	Dominican Republic	17,799
82	Costa Rica	17,645
83	Iraq	17,510
84	Serbia	17,404
85	North Macedonia	16,359
86	Brazil	16,068
87	Grenada	15,717
88	Algeria	15,622
89	Surinam	15,498
90	Maldives	15,312
91	Nauru	15,045
92	Colombia	14,999
93	Peru	14,393
94	Bosnia and Herzegovina	14,348
95	Saint Lucia	13,887
96	Mongolia	13,735
97	South Africa	13,730
98	Paraguay	13,571
99	Sri Lanka	13,450
100	Albania	13,326
101	Lebanon	13,058
102	Indonesia	13,057
103	Tunisia	12,484
104	Egypt	12,390
105	Saint Vincent and the Grenadines	12,307
106	Ecuador	11,714
107	Georgia	11,421
108	Republic of Kosovo	11,368
109	Namibia	11,135
110	Fiji	11,004
111	Eswatini	10,722
112	Dominica	10,650
113	Bhutan	10,516
114	Armenia	10,325
115	Jordan	9,348
116	Jamaica	9,299
117	Ukraine	9,233
118	Philippines	8,935
119	Belize	8,786
120		8,587
121	Guyana	8,569
122	Guatemala	8,447
123	El Salvador	8,317
124	Bolivia	7,859

#	Country	2018
125	India	7,762
126	East Timor	7,645
127	Cabo Verde	7,495
128	Laos	7,441
129	Vietnam	7,435
130	Moldova	7,301
131	Uzbekistan	7,020
132	Samoa	6,850
133	Myanmar	6,662
134	Angola	6,441
135	Tonga	6,408
136	Nigeria	5,980
137	Republic of Congo	5,652
138	Pakistan	5,544
139	Nicaragua	5,524
140	State of Palestine	5,148
141	Honduras	5,130
142	Sudan	4,759
143	Ghana	4,738
144	Bangladesh	4,364
145	Cambodia	4,354
146	Papua New Guinea	4,299
147	Zambia	4,216
148	Côte d'Ivoire	4,200
149	Mauritania	4,190
150	Marshall Islands	4,048
151	Tuvalu	4,042
152	Kyrgyzstan	3,878
153	Senegal	3,776
154	Cameroon	3,771
155	Micronesia	3,596
156	Kenya	3,461
157	Tajikistan	3,444
158	Sao Tome and Principe	3,413
159	Tanzania	3,227
160	Lesotho	3,223
161	Vanuatu	3,202
162	Nepal	3,064
163	Zimbabwe	3,024
164	Comoros	2,828
165	Guinea	2,630
166	Yemen	2,571
167	Benin	2,420
168	Solomon Islands	2,409
169	Mali	2,313
170	Kiribati	2,290
171	Rwanda	2,254

(Continued)

(Continued)

#	Country	2018
172	Uganda	2,033
173	Ethiopia	2,019
174	Burkina Faso	1,975
175	Chad	1,965
176	Afghanistan	1,952
177	Haiti	1,863
178	Guinea-Bissau	1,796
179	Togo	1,761
180	The Gambia	1,706
181	Madagascar	1,634
182	Sierra Leone	1,604
183	Mozambique	1,328
184	Malawi	1,309
185	Liberia	1,306
186	Niger	1,048
187	Democratic Republic of Congo	931
188	Central African Republic	872
189	Burundi	743

Human Development Index (UN Development Program)

#	Country	HDI
1	Norway	0.954
2	Switzerland	0.946
3	Ireland	0.942
4	Germany	0.939
4	Hong Kong	0.939
6	Australia	0.938
6	Iceland	0.938
8	Sweden	0.937
9	Singapore	0.935
10	Netherlands	0.933
11	Denmark	0.930
12	Finland	0.925
13	Canada	0.922
14	New Zealand	0.921
15	United Kingdom	0.920
15	United States of America	0.920
17	Belgium	0.919
18	Liechtenstein	0.917
19	Japan	0.915
20	Austria	0.914
21	Luxembourg	0.909
22	Israel	0.906

#	Country	HDI
22	Republic of Korea	0.906
24	Slovenia	0.902
25	Spain	0.893
26	Czech Republic	0.891
27	France	0.891
28	Malta	0.885
29	Italy	0.883
30	Estonia	0.882
31	Cyprus	0.873
32	Greece	0.872
32	Poland	0.872
34	Lithuania	0.869
35	United Arab Emirates	0.866
36	Andorra	0.857
36	Saudi Arabia	0.857
36	Slovakia	0.857
39	Latvia	0.854
40	Portugal	0.850
41	Qatar	0.848
42	Chile	0.847
43	Brunei	0.845
43	Hungary	0.845
45	Bahrain	0.838
46	Croatia	0.837
47	Oman	0.834
48	Argentina	0.830
49	Russia	0.824
50	Belarus	0.817
50	Kazakhstan	0.817
52	Bulgaria	0.816
52	Montenegro	0.816
52	Romania	0.816
55	Palau	0.814
56	Barbados	0.813
57	Kuwait	0.808
57	Uruguay	0.808
59	Turkey	0.806
60	Bahamas	0.805
61	Malaysia	0.804
62	Seychelles	0.801
63	Serbia	0.799
63	Trinidad and Tobago	0.799
65	Iran	0.797
66	Mauritius	0.796
67	Panama	0.795
68	Costa Rica	0.794
69	Albania	0.791

(Continued)

(Continued)

#	Country	HDI
70	Georgia	0.786
71	Sri Lanka	0.780
72	Cuba	0.778
73	Saint Kitts and Nevis	0.777
74	Antigua and Barbuda	0.776
75	Bosnia and Herzegovina	0.769
76	Mexico	0.767
77	Thailand	0.765
78	Grenada	0.763
79	Brazil	0.761
79	Colombia	0.761
81	Armenia	0.760
82	Algeria	0.759
82	North Macedonia	0.759
82	Peru	0.759
85	China	0.758
85	Ecuador	0.758
87	Azerbaijan	0.754
88	Ukraine	0.750
89	Dominican Republic	0.745
89	Saint Lucia	0.745
91	Tunisia	0.739
92	Mongolia	0.735
93	Lebanon	0.730
94	Botswana	0.728
94	Saint Vincent and the Grenadines	0.728
96	Jamaica	0.726
96	Venezuela	0.726
98	Dominica	0.724
98	Fiji	0.724
98	Paraguay	0.724
98	Surinam	0.724
102	Jordan	0.723
103	Belize	0.720
104	Maldives	0.719
105	Tonga	0.717
106	Philippines	0.712
107	Moldova	0.711
108	Turkmenistan	0.710
108	Uzbekistan	0.710
110	Libya	0.708
111	Indonesia	0.707
111	Samoa	0.707
113	South Africa	0.705
114	Bolivia	0.703
115	Gabon	0.702

#	Country	HDI
116	Egypt	0.700
117	Marshall Islands	0.698
118	Vietnam	0.693
119	Palestine	0.690
120	Iraq	0.689
121	Morocco	0.676
122	Kyrgyzstan	0.674
123	Guyana	0.670
124	El Salvador	0.667
125	Tajikistan	0.656
126	Cabo Verde	0.651
126	Guatemala	0.651
126	Nicaragua	0.651
129	India	0.647
130	Namibia	0.645
131	Timor-Leste	0.626
132	Honduras	0.623
132	Kiribati	0.623
134	Bhutan	0.617
135	Bangladesh	0.614
135	Micronesia	0.614
137	Sao Tome and Principe	0.609
138	Congo	0.608
138	Swaziland	0.608
140	Laos	0.604
141	Vanuatu	0.597
142	Ghana	0.596
143	Zambia	0.591
144	Equatorial Guinea	0.588
145	Myanmar	0.584
146	Cambodia	0.581
147	Kenya	0.579
147	Nepal	0.579
149	Angola	0.574
150	Cameroon	0.563
150	Zimbabwe	0.563
152	Pakistan	0.560
153	Solomon Islands	0.557
154	Syria	0.549
155	Papua New Guinea	0.543
156	Comoros	0.538
157	Rwanda	0.536
158	Nigeria	0.534
159	Tanzania	0.528
159	Uganda	0.528
161	Mauritania	0.527
162	Madagascar	0.521

(*Continued*)

(Continued)

#	Country	HDI
163	Benin	0.520
164	Lesotho	0.518
165	Côte d'Ivoire	0.516
166	Senegal	0.514
167	Togo	0.513
168	Sudan	0.507
169	Haiti	0.503
170	Afghanistan	0.496
171	Djibouti	0.495
172	Malawi	0.485
173	Ethiopia	0.470
174	The Gambia	0.466
174	Guinea	0.466
176	Liberia	0.465
177	Yemen	0.463
178	Guinea-Bissau	0.461
179	Democratic Republic of Congo	0.459
180	Mozambique	0.446
181	Sierra Leone	0.438
182	Burkina Faso	0.434
182	Eritrea	0.434
184	Mali	0.427
185	Burundi	0.423
186	South Sudan	0.413
187	Chad	0.401
188	Central African Republic	0.381
189	Niger	0.377

Fragile States Index (Fund for Peace)

#	Country	Index
1	Yemen	113.5
2	Somalia	112.3
3	South Sudan	112.2
4	Syria	111.5
5	Democratic Republic of Congo	110.2
6	Central African Republic	108.9
7	Chad	108.5
8	Sudan	108.0
9	Afghanistan	105.0
10	Zimbabwe	99.5
11	Guinea	99.4
12	Haiti	99.3
13	Iraq	99.1

#	Country	Index
14	Nigeria	98.5
15	Burundi	98.2
16	Cameroon	97.0
17	Eritrea	96.4
18	Niger	96.2
19	Guinea-Bissau	95.5
20	Uganda	95.3
21	Mali	94.5
22	Myanmar	94.3
23	Pakistan	94.2
23	Ethiopia	94.2
25	Kenya	93.5
26	North Korea	92.7
27	Congo	92.5
28	Libya	92.2
29	Côte d'Ivoire	92.1
30	Liberia	90.2
31	Mauritania	90.1
32	Venezuela	89.3
33	Mozambique	88.7
34	Egypt	88.4
35	Angola	87.8
36	Bangladesh	87.7
37	Rwanda	87.5
38	Togo	87.4
39	Sierra Leone	86.8
40	Zambia	85.7
41	Timor-Leste	85.5
42	Swaziland	85.3
43	Djibouti	85.1
44	Lebanon	85.0
45	Nepal	84.7
46	Sri Lanka	84.0
47	The Gambia	83.9
47	Burkina Faso	83.9
49	Malawi	83.3
50	Philippines	83.1
50	Papua New Guinea	83.1
52	Iran	83.0
53	Equatorial Guinea	82.6
54	Cambodia	82.5
55	Solomon Islands	81.9
56	Comoros	81.7
57	Guatemala	81.4
58	Madagascar	80.9
59	Turkey	80.3
60	Tanzania	80.1

(*Continued*)

(Continued)

#	Country	Index
61	Lesotho	79.7
62	Laos	78.7
63	Nicaragua	78.1
64	Honduras	77.8
65	Tajikistan	77.7
66	Senegal	77.2
67	Palestine	76.5
68	Kyrgyzstan	76.2
69	Jordan	75.9
70	Uzbekistan	75.7
70	Colombia	75.7
72	Algeria	75.4
73	Russia	74.7
74	India	74.4
75	Benin	73.6
76	Azerbaijan	73.2
77	Thailand	73.1
78	Morocco	73.0
78	Micronesia	73.0
80	Bolivia	72.9
81	Georgia	72.0
81	Bhutan	72.0
83	Brazil	71.8
84	Fiji	71.7
85	Turkmenistan	71.4
86	Bosnia and Herzegovina	71.3
87	Ecuador	71.2
88	South Africa	71.1
88	Sao Tome and Principe	71.1
88	China	71.1
91	Ukraine	71.0
92	Gabon	70.5
93	Saudi Arabia	70.4
93	Indonesia	70.4
95	Tunisia	70.1
96	Maldives	69.8
96	El Salvador	69.8
98	Mexico	69.7
99	Peru	68.2
99	Guyana	68.2
99	Belarus	68.2
102	Serbia	68.0
103	Moldova	67.1
104	Paraguay	67.0
105	Armenia	66.7
106	Cabo Verde	66.6

#	Country	Index
107	Namibia	66.4
108	Dominican Republic	66.2
109	Vietnam	66.1
110	Ghana	65.9
111	North Macedonia	64.6
112	Samoa	64.2
113	Bahrain	63.8
114	Belize	62.5
115	Surinam	61.9
116	Kazakhstan	61.6
117	Jamaica	61.2
118	Cuba	60.8
119	Malaysia	60.5
120	Botswana	59.5
121	Albania	58.9
122	Cyprus	57.8
123	Grenada	57.6
124	Brunei	57.5
125	Montenegro	55.3
126	Seychelles	55.2
127	Antigua and Barbuda	54.4
128	Mongolia	54.1
129	Greece	53.9
130	Kuwait	53.2
131	Trinidad and Tobago	53.0
132	Bulgaria	50.6
133	Oman	50.0
134	Hungary	49.6
135	Bahamas	48.8
136	Barbados	48.0
137	Romania	47.8
138	Croatia	47.5
139	Panama	47.0
140	Argentina	46.0
141	Qatar	45.4
142	Latvia	43.9
143	Italy	43.8
144	Poland	42.8
145	Costa Rica	42.0
146	Estonia	40.8
147	Spain	40.7
148	Slovakia	40.5
149	United Arab Emirates	40.1
150	Mauritius	38.9
150	Chile	38.9
152	Lithuania	38.1
153	United States of America	38.0

(Continued)

(Continued)

#	Country	Index
154	Czech Republic	37.6
155	United Kingdom	36.7
156	Malta	34.5
157	Japan	34.3
158	Uruguay	34.0
159	Republic of Korea	33.7
160	France	32.0
161	Belgium	28.6
162	Singapore	28.1
163	Slovenia	28.0
164	Portugal	25.3
165	Austria	25.0
166	Netherlands	24.8
167	Germany	24.7
168	Ireland	20.6
169	Luxembourg	20.4
170	Sweden	20.3
171	New Zealand	20.1
172	Canada	20.0
173	Iceland	19.8
174	Australia	19.7
175	Denmark	19.5
176	Switzerland	18.7
177	Norway	18.0
178	Finland	16.9

Ease of Doing Business Index (World Bank)

#	Country
1	New Zealand
2	Singapore
3	SAR Hong Kong, China
4	Denmark
5	Republic of Korea
6	United States of America
7	Georgia
8	United Kingdom
9	Norway
10	Sweden
11	Lithuania
12	Malaysia
13	Mauritius
14	Australia
15	Taiwan, China

#	Country
16	United Arab Emirates
17	North Macedonia
18	Estonia
19	Latvia
20	Finland
21	Thailand
22	Germany
23	Canada
24	Ireland
25	Kazakhstan
26	Iceland
27	Austria
28	Russia
29	Japan
30	Spain
31	China
32	France
33	Turkey
34	Azerbaijan
35	Israel
36	Switzerland
37	Slovenia
38	Rwanda
39	Portugal
40	Poland
41	Czech Republic
42	Netherlands
43	Bahrain
44	Serbia
45	Slovakia
46	Belgium
47	Armenia
48	Moldova
49	Belarus
50	Montenegro
51	Croatia
52	Hungary
53	Morocco
54	Cyprus
55	Romania
56	Kenya
57	Kosovo
58	Italy
59	Chile
60	Mexico
61	Bulgaria
62	Saudi Arabia

(*Continued*)

(Continued)

#	Country
63	India
64	Ukraine
65	Puerto Rico
66	Brunei
67	Colombia
68	Oman
69	Uzbekistan
70	Vietnam
71	Jamaica
72	Luxembourg
73	Indonesia
74	Costa Rica
75	Jordan
76	Peru
77	Qatar
78	Tunisia
79	Greece
80	Kyrgyzstan
81	Mongolia
82	Albania
83	Kuwait
84	South Africa
85	Zambia
86	Panama
87	Botswana
88	Malta
89	Bhutan
90	Bosnia and Herzegovina
91	El Salvador
92	San Marino
93	Saint Lucia
94	Nepal
95	Philippines
96	Guatemala
97	Togo
98	Samoa
99	Sri Lanka
100	Seychelles
101	Uruguay
102	Fiji
103	Tonga
104	Namibia
105	Trinidad and Tobago
106	Tajikistan
107	Vanuatu
108	Pakistan

#	Country
109	Malawi
110	Côte d'Ivoire
111	Dominica
112	Djibouti
113	Antigua and Barbuda
114	Egypt
115	Dominican Republic
116	Uganda
117	West Bank and Gaza
118	Ghana
119	Bahamas
120	Papua New Guinea
121	Eswatini
122	Lesotho
123	Senegal
124	Brazil
125	Paraguay
126	Argentina
127	Iran
128	Barbados
129	Ecuador
130	Saint Vincent and the Grenadines
131	Nigeria
132	Niger
133	Honduras
134	Guyana
135	Belize
136	Solomon Islands
137	Cabo Verde
138	Mozambique
139	Saint Kitts and Nevis
140	Zimbabwe
141	Tanzania
142	Nicaragua
143	Lebanon
144	Cambodia
145	Palau
146	Grenada
147	Maldives
148	Mali
149	Benin
150	Bolivia
151	Burkina Faso
152	Mauritania
153	Marshall Islands
154	Laos
155	The Gambia

(*Continued*)

110 *Auxiliary materials*

(Continued)

#	Country
156	Guinea
157	Algeria
158	Micronesia
159	Ethiopia
160	Comoros
161	Madagascar
162	Surinam
163	Sierra Leone
164	Kiribati
165	Myanmar
166	Burundi
167	Cameroon
168	Bangladesh
169	Gabon
170	Sao Tome and Principe
171	Sudan
172	Iraq
173	Afghanistan
174	Guinea-Bissau
175	Liberia
176	Syria
177	Angola
178	Equatorial Guinea
179	Haiti
180	Republic of Congo
181	East Timor (Timor-Leste)
182	Chad
183	Democratic Republic of Congo
184	Central African Republic
185	South Sudan
186	Libya
187	Yemen
188	Venezuela
189	Eritrea
190	Somalia
	Liechtenstein*

Index

Taylor & Francis Group
an **informa** business

Taylor & Francis eBooks

www.taylorfrancis.com

A single destination for eBooks from Taylor & Francis
with increased functionality and an improved user
experience to meet the needs of our customers.

90,000+ eBooks of award-winning academic content in
Humanities, Social Science, Science, Technology, Engineering,
and Medical written by a global network of editors and authors.

TAYLOR & FRANCIS EBOOKS OFFERS:

A streamlined
experience for
our library
customers

A single point
of discovery
for all of our
eBook content

Improved
search and
discovery of
content at both
book and
chapter level

REQUEST A FREE TRIAL
support@taylorfrancis.com

Routledge
Taylor & Francis Group

CRC Press
Taylor & Francis Group

For Product Safety Concerns and Information please contact our EU
representative GPSR@taylorandfrancis.com
Taylor & Francis Verlag GmbH, Kaufingerstraße 24, 80331 München, Germany

www.ingramcontent.com/pod-product-compliance
Lightning Source LLC
Chambersburg PA
CBHW061753270326
41928CB00011B/2486

* 9 7 8 0 3 6 7 6 4 1 8 4 9 *